Also by Dave Hop

Top Stories – 31 parables retold with c
Pulp Gospel – 31 bits of the Bible r
Rebel Yell: 31 Psalms – Psalms,
The Bloke's Bible – Bits of the B
The Bloke's Bible 2: The Road Tri,
Sons of Thunder – A contemporary gospel
No More Heroes – Cain, Solomon & Jacob in a modern
tale of men, women, dads and crime

Film &

Faith

Written, edited and directed by
Dave Hopwood

Starring a cast of 1000s

Movie Clips for your Church Events,
Small Groups and Personal Reflection

The pre-credit sequence...

My guess is this - if Jesus was around today he might well say something like, 'The kingdom of God is like a man who put on a red pair of tights and a spider's costume and jumped from one building to another...' I believe God is always speaking, and I believe he loves to communicate with us. Movies are just one way - but they are a very effective one.

In one sense there's nothing new about using contemporary media to communicate the nature of God's kingdom, there's nothing gimmicky about using stories to challenge our thinking. Jesus did it, so did the prophets; the guys who penned the psalms used anecdotal images, and a whole bunch of other Biblical writers followed suit. The Bible is crow-barred full of images and stories that we encounter again and again in life, books, TV, adverts and movies.

Jesus's famous parable of the good Samaritan is really just an episode of casualty, the story of the prodigal son happens every day in families up and down the country. We encounter the book of Job in our newspapers every time someone's life falls apart and Paul's image of the armour of God is just a scene nicked from *Gladiator*.

So here's a collection of mini parables for you. Sixty-six in fact; which coincidentally happens to be the same number as there are books in the Bible. I haven't tried to explain the theology behind each film, I've not tried to read the minds of the writers or directors. I've simply used each short scene as a jumping off point. This is one of the ways I learn more about God and his world these days, through a two-minute scene. Though I confess that it's terribly presumptuous to make such grand claims - perhaps I can at least say these clips help me to continue to work out what my faith might mean in this 21st Century world.

Feel free to use this book any way you like. The clips described may make you think of other issues. You may find your own clips that better illustrate the thoughts I've described. You may want to show more of the movie than I've described, or you may just want to describe the clip without showing it at all.

You may want to use the clips in your church, house group, evangelistic event, or personal quiet time. I began doing this kind of work after using a book called *Praying the Movies* by Edward McNulty in my daily reflection.

I've described the location of each clip as well as I can. Apologies if any timings are adrift. The timings begin from the moment the film opens, whether it's with a logo, or credit sequence or straight into the action. So whiz past all those trailers before you start the clock. I've also tried to warn you if the clips contain any swearing, you must then decide if that will offend your chosen audience.
If you show clips in public it's important to find out how you stand legally. Licenses can be obtained from CCL - it's worth talking to The Bible Society or CPAS. There is also something called Fair Use Exception. I leave you to wade through the grey porridge of it all.

Thanks for buying this book, and thank you to all those who helped me get my muddled thoughts on paper, not least Lynn, Ben, Justin & Delana. This book is dedicated to them, and to Tim Norton, who suggested one day that I start using video clips to help people think about the Bible. Thanks Tim, my life has never been the same since.

Index

Title: Pleasantville - Fires And Finn

Theme: The Incarnation

Bible references: John 1 vv 1-18; Philippians 2 vv 5-12: 1 John 1 vv 1-3

Location of clip: 48 mins 52 secs to 52 mins 32 secs

Film Description:
Bud loves 50's TV show *Pleasantville*. Life there is cleaner, brighter, safer, much more pleasant than life today. People are kinder, they do not swear and there is little violence. When Bud and his sister are given an unusual TV remote control gun it enables them to enter the TV and step into the show as characters. But Bud and his sister then make an interesting discovery. Life in Pleasantville may be rosy on the surface – but that's all there is to it – the surface. It has no depth. It is shiny but shallow. There is an impressive library in the town, but open a book and there is nothing inside because people don't read books on 50's TV shows. Visit the bathroom and you'll find there is no toilet – people would never do *that* in such a pleasant place. Bud inadvertently begins to lead some of the folk into a deeper life, a life with new things – passion, anger, frustration, creativity, love and colour. A broader, more complex life.

Clip Description:
Bud arrives at the coffee shop where he is now working to find the place full of inquisitive students. The previous night Bud put out a fire that was blazing in a tree outside his house. The fire brigade were at a loss to know how to deal with the crisis as their usual callout is to rescue cats from rooftops. In fact, Bud has to cry out 'Cat!' in order to get them to leave their seats in the fire station, shouting out 'Fire!' meant nothing to them at all.

Pleasantville is a perfectly pleasant place, nothing shocking or frightening ever normally happens there. Fires just don't occur.
In the coffee shop the students want to know how Bud knew about coping with such disasters.
Bud cautiously explains that he learnt this skill in the place where he used to live, a place where the roads don't just go around in circles, where rivers and highways run on forever. The students' eyes nearly pop, this is unknown territory to them.
One student presents Bud with a copy of *The Adventures of Huckleberry Finn*. Bud flips through the pages, there is nothing on them. The books in Pleasantville are all empty inside their covers, they are just for show because no one really needs to use these things.
Bud slowly explains what happens at the end of the book, as he does so the pages fill up with words. Life in Pleasantville is changing, it will never

1

be the same again.

Thoughts:
Bud has stepped into Pleasantville from another world, from a place that is utterly different and beyond the comprehension of those in Pleasantville. Bud opens their eyes to a world they never knew existed.

So did Jesus. He stepped in from another world, a world so different from ours. In fact as I read the gospels I can often see him standing there racking his brains thinking, 'Okay, these people have no comprehension about this particular principal of the kingdom of God, how am I going to explain this one to them?'

Jesus came from a place so different to ours with the express purpose of introducing us to that world. A place of space, a place where the roads go on forever, a place where other things are possible, things currently beyond our experience or comprehension.
But like Bud he was cautious, he dressed his descriptions of the new kingdom in parables and called them secrets. He protected this costly knowledge so that those who would deride him could only scoff at his storytelling, they were not able to laugh at the precious pearls of the kingdom. He deliberately expressed the new principals in ways that required relationship with him, demanded dialogue, conversation with the Son of God.

In Pleasantville, as the occupants discover real things, like passion, anger, desire, love, ambition, their lives change from black and white to colour. So it is with the kingdom of God. For those with the courage to listen to and interact with the Storyteller, their lives will adopt all kinds of shades, some light, some dark, divine colours that will change them and their world forever.

Questions:
1. Can you describe any experiences that have happened to you as a Christian, which, before following Jesus, would have been beyond your comprehension?
2. Are there any ways in which you find the other-worldliness of Jesus disturbing?
3. How can we help each other to keep that sense of wonder about the kingdom of God?
4. Jesus upset a few people, as Bud did in Pleasantville; how do you feel about the possibilities of upsetting others as you follow Jesus?
5. Did the clip make you think about anything else?

Film title: Kill Bill Vol 2 – Stories And Suspense

Themes: Jesus – the master communicator, shocking, surprising, enigmatic and provocative; how may we communicate the good news?

Bible references: Mark 12 vv 1-12

Location of clip: 37 mins 37 secs to 41 mins 10 secs

Description of film:
The Bride is seeking revenge on her former lover Bill and his henchmen and women. Bill has taught the Bride all she knows about life. But when she leaves him, and attempts to start a knew life, he tracks her down and tries to kill her at her wedding. As a result of the attack, The Bride spends months in a coma. When she finally wakes, she begins to track down those who wished her dead. She makes a list and one by one she picks them off. During the telling of this murderous tale we see flashbacks into The Bride's past with Bill. This clip is one of those flashbacks.

Description of clip:
Bill and the Bride sit around a campfire at night. Bill tells her a story about *The five finger exploding heart technique*. (N.B. possibly a useful device for dealing with traffic wardens and those who take eleven items into the *ten items or less* queue in the supermarket.) He tells her the story of Pae Mei. It is a story of insult and revenge, a story of retribution and violence. As Bill tells the tale he pauses frequently to play his flute, his voice is slow and steady, keeping the Bride hanging on his every word.

Thoughts:
Bill is a consummate storyteller - a man who knows how to draw his audience in. As you watch The Bride it's quite clear she is quickly enveloped in his tale of honour and retribution. He pauses at the cliff-hanger moments, drops his voice to encourage her to come closer, stops every now and then to play his flute and keep her hanging on for the next thrilling instalment.
I think this is how Jesus must have told stories.
In a culture where parables were regularly used to pass on wisdom and teaching, Jesus took the medium of his day and gave it an extra spin. His tales were full of courage and crime, twists and turns, heroes and villains, and sometimes - violence.

When I first saw this clip and considered using it to help people think about Jesus the storyteller, I wondered whether it would be appropriate; Bill's tale ends violently, with a massacre in a temple. A little unpalatable

3

perhaps. Or is it? I once reflected on the notion that, had Jesus attempted to get a publisher for a collection of his stories, a sort of *Best Of* compilation, some Christian publishers might well have requested he tone down the content of some of his tales. Not least the violence in The Good Samaritan (perhaps the traveller could have just been jostled, rather than abused and assaulted); the massacre that ends the story about the workers in the vineyard is surely gratuitous and unnecessary; so too the heavy-handed punishment for the poor gate-crasher in the Parable of the Banquet, and yet again at the end of the Parable of the Talents....

And so it goes on. Jesus's stories were not necessarily the nice childhood tales we sometimes think they are. We have become familiar with many of them and they have lost their cutting edge. Samaritans were once perceived as despicable people, perhaps like members of al-Qaeda today; nowadays the Samaritans are a benevolent organisation you can call when feeling depressed or suicidal.

And the same is true for many familiar Old Testament stories, perhaps we draw the teeth on some of these tales when we grow up hearing them told as if they are something off children's TV. It warms my heart whenever I hear Bible readings delivered with thought and talent, not read as if they are the weather forecast, but presented like Bill tells a story, with style, passion, wit and confidence.

There is another reason for taking care in communicating the gospel. We quickly forget what it is like to be outside the kingdom. What once seemed to us as odd, quirky and downright embarrassing is now full of hope, purpose and acceptance. Not so for those still on the outside. What we wave about as good news, they may well see as a sword or hear as a car alarm. People need to be wooed, intrigued, respected and entertained. They are easily put off. *The Shawshank Redemption* is now one of the most popular movies of all time – yet no one went to see it when it first hit cinemas. It is likely they were put off by one single word in the title (a film-maker's nightmare) – *Redemption*. It sounds religious, it sounds worthy, it sounds preachy.

When Ezekiel was briefed by God to act out his message for the people God gave him this instruction – 'When the people ask you what you are doing – tell them.'

When they ask you... In other words don't just bandy this stuff about like free sweets, wet people's appetite, guard the secrets of the kingdom, wrap them up in parables and mystery, keep your pearls from the swine.

Questions:
1. Which of Jesus's stories do you love best? Why?
2. Have you ever squirmed at heavy-handed or inappropriate evangelism?

3. How can we help people to stay awake when the Bible reading comes around in church?
4. Can you remember what it was like to be outside the kingdom, not understanding the Christian message? What drew you closer?
5. Did the clip make you think about anything else?

Film Title: The Untouchables – God Calls Nobodies

Theme: God uses our experience & personality, the raw material of our lives

Bible references: Exodus 3 & 4; 1 Corinthians 12 vv 7-10

Location of clip: 22 mins to 24 mins 20 secs

Description of film:
It is 1930s America, a time of gangsters, guns and illegal alcohol. Elliot Ness is a treasury officer in Chicago who forms a small band of honest men to fight the corruption in the system. Prohibition outlaws the sale of alcohol, yet the industry thrives – because everyone is taking money to turn a blind eye. If Elliot Ness is to make any difference he must break away from the established forces of law and order and form his own band of trustworthy men.

Description of clip:
Elliot goes to visit Jim Malone, an ordinary, ageing cop, still walking the beat after many years in the force. The two have met previously and Elliot can see that Malone is morally decent and committed to upholding the law. Elliot unveils his plan to create a small force, committed to fighting the corruption in the system and breaking the power of Al Capone. Few men can be trusted, even the police are making money through secret deals and blind eyes turned. Elliot wants to change all this.
Jim Malone is having none of it. He's old, he's near retirement, while he might once have jumped at the chance, now he just wants to stay alive. He understands the problem, he wishes they could do something, but he also wishes Ness had turned up '10 years and 20 pounds ago...' He's past it. 'It's just become too important to stay alive...'
Yet Ness can see that Malone's experience and his approach to life are just what he needs to do this dangerous job.

Thoughts:
There is a prevailing idea that if we were just a little more spiritual, if we were better Christians, God would use us more. When I look at the Biblical heroes I don't see that principle at work. Not at all. Jesus didn't pick the disciples because they were exceptionally spiritual. God didn't select Moses (or Joseph, or Samson, or Peter) because he was particularly good at praying. As far as we know - intercession wasn't particularly high on his *to do* list.

God called Moses because of his life experience. He'd lived in the

Egyptian Royal family for decades, he had relatives in the Jewish quarter. And of course, he knew the desert like the back of his hand.

One problem, like Jim Malone, Moses thought his life was over, he thought he'd had his glory days and was practically retired. At one time he had been enthusiastic, reckless - now he must have wondered if he was exiled in the desert living under God's curse because he had fled Egypt under sentence of death. He was a murderer. In those days if you were in crisis it was often seen as punishment from God. Yet just the opposite was true.

Moses had been in training for eighty years and he didn't know it. When God turns up, Moses more or less says, 'You should have come 40 years and 20 pounds ago. I was enthusiastic then. I wanted to change the world. Now I'm just tired and scared.'

He was probably also worried about the prison food waiting for him, should he ever venture back onto Egyptian sand.

Yet God won't be flannelled by this. He sees that Moses has just the right qualifications for this job. He'll keep pushing until Moses gives in.

Moses serves up the excuses and God has a return for every one. It's almost as if he's saying 'Those very things you feel disqualify you – they are just the things that make you perfect for the job. You thought you could change things when you were younger. Now you think you can't. Perfect. You're a blank canvas, you're ready now. You've spent 40 years leading sheep across the desert, well – now I have a lot more sheep for you to lead across the desert...'

God cared deeply for Moses, there were very few people, then or now, with the depths of integrity and humility that Moses possessed. God's calling on his life was deeply tied up in Moses's personality and life experience. God doesn't even seem that bothered that Moses isn't talented in speaking out the message. It's Moses who has to point this out to God. God's barely noticed.

A friend once said to me, 'Moses spent his first 40 years as a prince thinking he was somebody, then the next 40 finding out he was actually nobody. And the last 40 discovering what God could do with a nobody.' You're not a spiritual giant, you're just a nobody. Now that's what I call good news...

Questions:

1. The Bible speaks of us as dust, as if God never overestimates our abilities. Are there ways in which we expect too much of ourselves? More than God expects?

2. Can you think of ways in which you are weak? Could God use those things?

3. What are you interested in? What does your personality and experience qualify you for?
4. A minister once told me that when he accompanied a friend to work he saw a different side to him than he had ever seen in church. Are you the same in church, as you are, say at work, or out with your friends, or shopping, or at school? If not, why?
5. Did the clip make you think about anything else?

Title: The Green Mile – The Power And The Glory

Themes: The power of God displayed through Elisha and Jesus, and people's reaction to this

Bible references: 2 Kings 4 vv 18-37; Matthew 9 vv18-26

Location of clip: 2 hours 9 mins to 2 hours 13 mins

Warning: This clip may contain swearing (depending on the point at which you begin)

Description of film:
John Coffey is on death row convicted of murder. He is a mountain of a man, overpowering, dangerous, mysterious. But the unexpected happens. This convicted killer begins to display supernatural healing power. One day he heals one of the guards, Paul Edgecomb; Paul has a friend whose wife is fatally ill. He begins to wonder if John Coffey might be able to help.

Description of clip:
Paul and the other guards take John Coffey to see the woman in the dead of night. They have to take John out of his cell secretly as he is not supposed to leave the prison. Slowly John Coffey enters her room. She is scared and delirious, she swears at him. Her husband is scared too. The whole nature of the visit is disturbing - armed guards arriving unannounced at midnight, accompanied by this huge black convict who does not appear to be under their control. No wonder there is fear in the air, it hangs like a clammy, poisonous mist in the woman's bedroom. John Coffey walks to the woman's sick bed. He towers over her, then sits down and talks to her gently. He reassures her, tells her his name, then he reaches down and places his mouth to hers. Power passes between them, he sucks the sickness from her. The house trembles, the clock face shatters, the lights flutter and flicker. And suddenly, as the tremors subside, she is okay. John Coffey stands and staggers back, reeling from the effects of healing her. She is relaxed now, smiling, the pain and the fever have gone. Her husband sits beside her, he smiles, talks gently, then breaks down and weeps.

Thoughts:
What must it have been like to have witnessed Jesus working miracles? The problem with the Bible is that these earth-shattering occasions pass in the space of five lines. We have the barest of details. Sometimes it must have been like this scene. We know that when Jesus died on the cross

graves opened up and relinquished corpses that had suddenly returned to life. Sounds like something from a horror film, doesn't it?

When Jesus went into the house of Jairus it was not a pretty scene, there was a dead girl on a bed and people laughing outside. We know now that it has a happy ending – but there must have been fear, confusion, doubt, stress… Jesus often stepped into situations that were fraught with tension. Hindsight's a wonderful thing – but it also blurs our vision when we consider what really happened. When Jesus reached out and brought life surging back through the girl's veins the house may well have shuddered, people may well have screamed, fainted, laughed and burst out with all kinds of words and phrases.

In the Old Testament there is a very similar scene to the one in the film. Elisha visits a house where a young boy lies dead on a bed. He places his lips to the boy's lips, places his body on the boy's, and literally breathes life back into him. It's startling stuff. The people witnessing these events must have had all kinds of reactions, sometimes there's a fine line between grief and happiness. Certainly there was much more happening than is recorded – there just wasn't the time or space to note it all I guess.

One thing's for sure – Jesus got intimately involved with those he healed. He touched them, he whispered, he sometimes used spit and mud, he held their hands, touched their eyes and ears, he lifted them up. He got, as they say, up close and personal.

Questions:
1. Do you think Jesus was ever saddened by the first response he encountered, say the ridiculing in this story, or the fear from the disciples when he appeared to them walking on the water?
2. Life around Jesus could well have been shocking, messy, stressful and surprising; does that appeal to you, or would you prefer a tidy life?
3. Jesus wept when he found his friend Lazarus dead. Why do you think that was? How do you think that made the disciples feel?
4. Which means more to you? The miracles of Jesus, or the parables? How about the meals he shares and the friendships he forms?
5. Did the clip make you think about anything else?

Title: Shrek – Speaking In Terms

Themes: Stripping away the pretence, being true to ourselves, bringing our humanity into our worship and witness

Bible references: Ezekiel 4 vv 12-17, John 1 vv 45-51, John 8 v 32

Location of clip: 25 mins to 27 mins

Description of film:
Shrek is an ogre. His swamp has been invaded by fairytale creatures on the run from the evil Lord Faquad. In order to get rid of these folklore squatters and regain the freedom of his swamp Shrek agrees to undertake a quest with Donkey to find a wife for the evil Lord Faquad. If he can rescue Princess Fiona from the prison where she is guarded by a fire-breathing dragon, and then bring her back to marry Lord Faquad, he will be free to return to his swamp and his life of ogre-ing.

Description of clip:
Shrek and Donkey are trekking through an onion field. As they walk Shrek eats and Donkey talks. Shrek brashly declares to Donkey that ogres are like onions - they have layers. Onions have layers - ogres have layers. But Donkey, his sensibilities offended by the comparison, tries to find a more pleasing alternative, a more palatable description. He offers the alternatives of cake or ice cream (parfait). Now that's much nicer. But Shrek is having none of it. He wants to tell the truth, not dress it up in fancy clothes. If he sees himself like an onion, he'll say that. He wants to tell it like it is.

Thoughts:
Have you ever noticed how we often use words and phrases in worship and evangelism that we rarely use in our normal life? Christians in church often speak of *joy* rather than happiness or excitement or pleasure. We *share* things with the congregation rather than simply telling them. We often use the words *really* and *just* to emphasise and punctuate our prayers. We sometimes adopt a certain tone of voice when praying aloud, or *sharing* our testimony. And when do we ever *share a testimony* in the rest of life?

We do not mention some subjects at all. For example we talk freely of sin – but never about sex. We talk about the things that God has sorted out in our lives, but not about the things which are still a mess. We tell of our successes, but not our failures.

11

We frequently err towards the fluffy, nice, ice cream and cake side of life, rather than the grubby, earthy, onion side of life.

Not so in the Bible.

When Paul speaks of our sins being like filthy rags he is referring to the cloths that the women of his day used when they were having their period. Graphic indeed.

If only we were aware of it.

There's a nice little exchange between Ezekiel and God in the Old Testament. God asks Ezekiel to cook some food over some human dung. Ezekiel is appalled – the food will be defiled and therefore Ezekiel will be sinning against God.

So God gives in and allows Ezekiel to cook over cow dung – still fairly unpleasant really, I haven't seen much manure on *Celebrity MasterChef* lately.

God seems to be prepared to go much further than Ezekiel in order to communicate with the people he loves. Ezekiel is worried about the outward form of things. God's bothered about sorting out the deeper issues. He is not so concerned about things looking clean and Christian.

Where's this all leading? Well, perhaps, when we try and sanitise the Bible and dress up our language in church, we are inadvertently sending out the message that God is only interested in nice people, and the nice things we do – when the opposite is true. We really don't have to pretend in front of God, we really don't. We can tell it like it is, we don't have to put on religious voices and use saintly-speak.

When Nathaniel first meets Jesus he is starstruck. Perhaps word had started to spread about this famous guy who could do anything. So, when Jesus says to him, 'I saw you under the tree, I've already spotted you…' like so many of us Nathaniel is wowed by the attention of someone famous. He blurts out, 'You really must be the Son of God!' Perhaps in the same way that, if I met Rowan Atkinson and he said, 'I've seen your book Dave. You write about films and the Bible.' I would probably reply, 'You are an incredibly talented and funny guy – you're a great actor. You must be special 'cause you're famous and you like me.' (Probably not out loud, but certainly in my head.)

Nathaniel is just starstruck, and Jesus can see through it. I imagine him cracking an ironic smile as he replies, 'You think I'm the Son of God 'cause I said I saw you under a tree? Easy tiger. You ain't seen nothing yet…'

We can be ourselves, and tell it like it is. That's surely what God really wants us to do.

Questions:

1. Do you find it difficult to tell the truth in church sometimes, for example if people ask you how you are doing?
2. Many modern worship songs speak of soft, nice things, like gentleness, peace and love. Do you think it might be possible to sing songs that are more similar to the Psalms, speaking of anger, fear, lament, and other more earthy things?
3. Do you think Shrek and Donkey would fit in at your church?
4. Consider this – if we only ever talk of the ways God has successfully sorted out the past, and rarely talk of him being with us in our everyday mess and failure, are we trying to somehow prove God's existence by passing on our own success stories?
5. Did the clip make you think about anything else?

Title: Dead Poets Society – We Read The Bible Because We're Alive

Theme: The Bible is a book full of real people living real lives

Bible refs: Matthew 13 v 11; Hebrews 11 vv 32 - 38

Location of clip: 20 mins 10 secs to 25 mins 40 secs

Film Description:

Mr Keating is an English and poetry teacher, but he doesn't teach like other teachers. He understands that the boys in his class are not really interested in poetry. So Mr Keating begins where they are. Like Jesus, he uses all kinds of devices and techniques to communicate what he loves and believes in. Poetry, and the love of it, oozes from Mr Keating and for some of the boys in his class, it will change their lives forever.

Clip Description:

In one of his first lessons with the boys he asks one of his pupils to read out the introduction to a poetry book by one Mr J Evans Pritchard. The boy painstakingly reads and describes how a person can decide whether a poem is good or bad by drawing a graph and plotting the poem's greatness on it.

Mr Keating demonstrates the graph on the board and at least one of the boys copies this down in his notebook. When the introduction is over Mr Keating turns to the class and carefully and deliberately says, 'Excrement.' Ripples of surprise spread through the ranks of desks.

Mr Keating is not at all impressed by Mr J Evans Pritchard's academic approach. Mr Evans has missed the point. You can't measure poetry with a ruler, you can't define it with scales or a tape measure. Poetry is about love, passion, fury, frustration, desire, joy and longing. Poetry is life itself. Mr Keating quotes from one poem after another as he impresses this upon the boys.

Thoughts:

I recommend that anyone involved in communicating the Bible should regularly watch *Dead Poets Society* – weekly if necessary.

Every time I see clips from this movie it opens my eyes afresh to the way Jesus must have taught.

Notice that Jesus did not tell many parables about carpentry or building – the world he knew and loved. He told parables about farming and fishing. That was the world of the ordinary people listening to him.

We need to begin where the audience are, just as Mr Keating and Jesus both do. Jesus understood how people tick, he understood that they need images, parables, puzzles, secrets and jokes to help them understand and

remember and wrestle with this thing that is the kingdom of God. They had completely the wrong idea about it. They had been conditioned by bad teaching and misunderstanding.
I wonder what conditioning we suffer from today.

The Bible is a book full of three-dimensional characters. People who were as mixed up and muddled as we are. Even great saints like Paul and Peter, Moses and David, Mary and Ruth. They all had good days and bad days. That's very good news! We can relate to them. They were complex, muddled, passionate people. Just like us.
The Bible is a book dripping with passion, courage, doubt, fear, frustration, fury and humanity. We must rediscover this, we must find ways to communicate this afresh. We must start with where the people are today.

Perhaps we have to rethink how we teach, how we communicate, how we share the stories. Perhaps we have to rediscover the stories for ourselves. Books such as *The Scandal of Grace* by Nick Baines and *Mark for Everyone* by Tom Wright are great places to begin the rediscovery.

In the clip Mr Keating tells the boys, 'We don't read poetry because it's cute, we read poetry because we are members of the human race...'
I would love to be able to say, 'I don't read the Bible because I'm a Christian, I read the Bible because I'm alive...'
Life, true life, honest life, muddled life... oozes from its pages.

Questions:
1. Can you recall a particular talk, sermon, drama or illustration which taught you something?
2. What conditioning do you suffer from? Have you considered this before?
3. Which Old Testament characters do you identify with?
4. How can we rediscover the reality within the Bible? How can we see these accounts with fresh eyes?
5. Did the clip make you think about anything else?

Title: The Passion - Jesus Was A Real Bloke

Theme: The Incarnation

Bible refs: Luke 2 v 52; Philippians 2 vv 5-8

Location of clip: 19 mins 7 secs to 20 mins 54 secs

Film Description:
'You must be the only person (in Jerusalem) who hasn't heard of this thing…'
It's tempting to misquote Luke 24 as I begin to describe this one. I doubt if there are many readers who have not heard of Mel Gibson's movie about the last hours of Jesus's pre-resurrection life on earth. Controversy and hype followed on the coat-tails of the release of this film. Personally, I can't see what the fuss was about. Perhaps we just forgot that at the heart of the Christian story about the need for forgiveness and redemption, there is an extremely violent, very bloody sacrifice.

This account majors on the torture and suffering that Jesus endured for us, and begins with the line from Isaiah, 'By his stripes we are healed.' Throughout the movie we are reminded that Jesus became a bloody collage of scars and stripes.
But tucked away there are some lovely flashbacks; Jesus is portrayed as caring, humorous, genuine and approachable.

Clip Description:
Jesus is making a table. His mother asks him if he's hungry. They discuss the table and the fact that it is higher than normal. Jesus explains that it is for a rich man and demonstrates by miming sitting on a chair at the table. This was unusual in those days and Jesus's mum remarks that it will never catch on. She tells him to wash his hands before eating and he splashes her with some of the water she is carrying in a bowl.

Thoughts:
Nothing remarkable happens really, but that's the point. Jesus must have had days that were ordinary, boring, tedious, not-that-entertaining, run-of-the-mill.
Jesus also had an incredible sense of humour, was very down-to-earth and was extremely approachable. Why else would the sick and the downtrodden and the young flock to him? They can't have been overpowered or overawed by him, can they?

We find it very difficult to imagine a man who is the son of God living an

16

ordinary life. We regularly see him portrayed in a divine nighty with a dazzling golden halo round his head, even as a baby. We sing about the fact that as a baby 'No crying he makes'. Utter dross I'm afraid to say. Actually, I'm not afraid at all, I'm pleased, he was real, not cardboard.

Jesus came to disclose the secrets of the kingdom to those with the eyes to see them. He came to draw people into relationship with God – so it's very unlikely that he would have telegraphed that fact by looking weird or otherworldly. Chances are he appeared a little rustic and a bit of a rookie. Why else would the religious leaders be shocked when they heard him sharing his wisdom. If he'd have sounded like Colin Firth or Rupert Everett no one would have been surprised at all. It's more likely he looked forgettable, able to blend in with the crowd, a Mr Everyman character.

We mustn't forget that Jesus would have sweated along with all the other men of his day. He had normal bodily functions and most likely had favourite foods, favourite memories of growing up, favourite ways that he chose to relax and conversation topics he enjoyed.

If Jesus had walked around with a benign smile on his face and his arms ever open people would have thought him a bit of a loony really. Instead he was man of reality, a man of dignity, a man of character and humour, an authentic man with great social skills.

I like to think of him too as a 'man's man', used to carpentry and building, calloused and sunburnt, well acquainted with the rigours of life and the rough and ready individuals who hung about on street corners. But it's clear too that he was compassionate, gentle and eloquent.

What about you? How do you see him?

Questions:
1. Do you imagine that Jesus was good-looking? Have a look at Isaiah 53 v 2.
2. Supposing he wasn't, does this matter to you?
3. We often talk of a relationship with Jesus, bearing in mind your relationships with other people what clues does these give you as to how your friendship with God might grow and develop?
4. Can you think of clues in the Bible which point to the true humanity of Jesus?
5. Did the clip make you think about anything else?

Title: Kill Bill Vol 2 – Grave Bustin'

Theme: The Resurrection of Jesus

Bible refs: John 20 vv 1-18

Location of clip: 55 mins 13 secs to 60 mins

Film Description:
The Bride is on the trail of the gang of criminals who attempted to kill her. Ultimately, as the title suggests, she intends to kill Bill, her former boyfriend, but in the meantime she must first bump off his henchmen and women. She has already dispensed with two of them and now comes to Budd, a.k.a. Sidewinder, to dispose of him next.

Clip Description:
The Bride has been drugged and kidnapped by Budd, he was ready for her when she came to his caravan. He slammed a hypodermic needle into her and tied her up. Now he has taken her to a cemetery and buried her alive. Instead of reeking revenge on him, she finds herself trapped inside a wooden coffin, buried deep underground. Surely there is no way out for her now. This must be the end.

But The Bride has been trained in the ancient martial arts and has the ability to break through the wood with her bear hands. As we watch she punches through the coffin lid and then continues to bust her way up through the earth and out of the grave into freedom. The music that plays adds to the sense of liberation, escape and freedom.

Thoughts:
The resurrection must surely be one of the most exhilarating moments in history. Yet time and again we fail to portray it in this light. Film-makers often treat it as a sterile moment devoid of laughter, passion, power or surprise.

The resurrection was a shocking occurrence. Easter Sunday dawned with the disciples feeling tired, depressed and on the verge of losing their faith. Mary probably had a bad headache and a sick stomach as she ventured towards the tomb after a sleepless night.

How can we recapture those moments of explosive life? This is especially difficult of course because we know they're coming. And personally I can't stand the well-rehearsed Easter morning ecclesiastical excitement that often takes place in church. Excitement isn't genuine if you're told to feel it.

18

Perhaps a parable is the best way to get a glimpse again, perhaps watching The Bride literally bust out of the grave is the closest we can come to seeing the new life break out, feeling the exhilaration of death itself being dealt the death blow.

In Martin Scorsese's *The Last Temptation* the raising of Lazarus is very well done indeed. It has power, suspense, a moment of shock, and a tangible sense of uncertainty as Jesus hovers in the grave doorway, having dispensed power which has seemingly had no effect.

There were only a couple of angels and two sleeping soldiers that morning at the tomb when the stone cracked in two and the whole of earth trembled under the footfall of a risen man. Unlike Christmas, which was announced in neon with angels and songs and breathless shepherds. The wise men heard about it halfway across the globe. But not the resurrection, perhaps this is something we can only really grasp on a personal level. But whatever the case – this was a momentous moment in history and deserves a little more than the dreary, 'The Lord is risen... (cough, shuffle)... He is risen indeed.'

Questions:
1. Sunday morning at the tomb must have been chaotic, all that panic over a lost body. Consider what happens when you have lost your keys. How often do you run back and forth like a headless chicken, searching the same place time and again to find them?
2. The gospel accounts vary as to what happened that morning and who did what, personally I think this adds to the argument that much confused activity was going on, what do you think?
3. How might we help one another to see again those earth-splintering moments of the resurrection?
4. Do you ever have problems with the resurrection? Have you spent much time thinking about it?
5. Did the clip make you think about anything else?

Title: Last Of The Mohicans – I Get Knocked Down…

Theme: Perseverance

Bible refs: 2 Corinthians 4 vv 8-12;

Location of clip: 1 hour 25 mins to 1 hour 27 mins 38 secs

Film Description:
The year is 1757. In the American colonies war is raging between England and France. The last remaining Mohicans, Chingachgook and his son Uncas and adopted son Hawkeye, have rescued Alice and Cora, the daughters of English Colonel Munro; and are escorting them to safety. Suddenly they are ambushed by a war party of Mohawks, led by the brutal Magua. Magua kidnaps the girls and takes them to the nearby Huron tribe, there to be burned alive, as trophies of the war. But Hawkeye and the others have not abandoned them. They are in pursuit, and as Magua bargains with the Huron chief, Hawkeye strides through the camp towards them.

Clip Description:
Walking tall, Hawkeye comes to set Cora and Alice free. Huron warriors stream towards him to stop him. Time and again they come at him, beating him with clubs, knocking him down, one of them cuts him with a knife. But Hawkeye barely sees them, he has his eyes fixed on the girls, he has his gaze set on the people he has come to set free. He has set his face towards the prize and nothing will deter him. No matter how many times he is knocked down by the Huron warriors, he gets up again and strides on towards the showdown. When he finally reaches Magua, the Huron chief and the girls he states his mission simply, 'Let the children of the dead Colonel Munro go free.' No messing, no debate. He is ready to make the sacrifice – himself in their place.

Thoughts:
As he neared the end of his three-year ministry Jesus pressed on towards the climactic clash in Jerusalem, one version of the Bible says, 'He set his face towards Jerusalem…'
I have images of Jesus turning, standing tall, striding towards that showdown with sin and death in the Holy City. Many people tried to stop him. The Pharisees tried to trick him, his own disciples tried to influence him, other religious leaders told lies about him and accused him of coming from the devil.
But nothing deterred him. He pressed on. Nothing could stop him from coming to set the children of the dead Adam and Eve free.

He must have had his dark moments of course. He must have wrestled in those wilderness places. It set me wondering recently when I thought again about Gethsemane. Only days before this Jesus had told his disciples, 'The son of man will be handed over to the gentiles, who will mock him, insult him and spit on him. They will whip him and kill him, but three days later he will rise to life.'
This was at least the third time Jesus had clearly outlined this plan to his friends. Yet on the night itself, on that grim, lonely night, as Jesus finds himself alone in the garden of Gethsemane, his theology crumbles a little. Though he knows well what he must do he prays that there might be another way. In the daylight he sees the plan clearly, in the dead of night he is frightened and depressed and he pleads for another plan.

This heartens me because so often I parade my theology in public, I boldly claim this and that about God in front of an audience. I talk about heaven and forgiveness and salvation and the loving father in the daylight. But at three in the morning, when it's dark and I can't sleep and I feel alone my theology often crumbles. The doubts creep in… no, that's an understatement, the doubts come at me like four walls closing in on me, about to crush me to death.
On one occasion Jesus asked his disciples that burning question, 'Who do the people say I am?' This was just after he'd been alone, talking to his father. Perhaps that had been a lonely time, perhaps on that particularly day he was tired of being misunderstood by the majority, tired of having to press on against the odds, tired of always having to swim against the tide of cynicism and unbelief…

Questions:
1. Had you ever considered that in order to empathise with and understand your dark moments of struggle and doubt, Jesus must have wrestled with his own similar struggles?
2. How can we help each other with these dark moments of doubt and fear? In 2 Corinthians 4 vv 8-12 Paul admits that even he often had doubts and was full of troubles. How can you best support your leaders, bearing in mind that they must often wrestle with their own faith?
3. Have you ever had moments when you were so inspired by your faith, that, like Hawkeye in the clip, nothing could you stop you from pressing forward and doing the right thing for God?
4. Are you facing opposition at the moment, at home, at work, at church? Are you having to battle against anything? Can you talk about it? Can you pray with anyone about it?
5. Did the clip make you think about anything else?

Title: Gladiator – That's My Boy!

Theme: Our status in God

Bible refs: Mark 1 vv 9-12

Location of clip: 1 hour 25 mins to 1 hour 28 mins

Film Description:

Maximus Decimus Meridius is a fine Roman General. Until the murder of his beloved Emperor Marcus Aurelius. Commodus, the emperor's son, kills his own father and Maximus falls out of favour, so out of favour that he is sentenced to death.

In a showdown in the forest Maximus kills his would-be executioners and flees for his life.

Commodus immediately orders the killing of Maximus's wife and child, along with the destruction of his home and estate.

So Maximus now has a single mission in mind, he must avenge the slaughter of his family and the murder of his beloved emperor. To do this he hides his true identity and becomes a gladiator. He trains with the others and waits for the day when he will fight before Commodus, the new, corrupt emperor. Once in the arena he will somehow engineer a face-to face meeting with Commodus so he can kill him.

Clip Description:

Maximus and his fellow gladiators have just won a shock victory in the arena. The scene was supposed to be a re-enactment of the battle of Carthage, which the Romans won convincingly. But in this case, under the leadership of Maximus, the 'barbarian' gladiators have turned the tide of history and smashed their Roman attackers.

The emperor is impressed. So impressed that he demands to meet this new gladiator. He steps into the arena and approaches Maximus.

Maximus is wearing a helmet with a visor so his identity, thus far, has been concealed. He is known only as The Spaniard.

It is only as Commodus meets him and demands he remove his helmet, that the truth is revealed. Maximus is alive! Commodus reels at the discovery as Maximus reveals his face and with clarity and determination states: 'My name is Maximus Decimus Meridius, Commander of the armies of the north, General of the Felix legions. Loyal servant to the true emperor, Marcus Aurelius. Father to a murdered son, husband to a murdered wife – and I will have my vengeance... in this life or the next.'

Thoughts:

Maximus knows who he is. He has had plenty of time to figure this out. He has spent difficult times training and preparing for this moment. He has lived a life of struggles and pleasure, victory, pain and loss – and now he knows who he is and what he must do. He is secure in his identity and his mission. So secure that he is willing to lay down his life for it.

We all need to know who we are and where we're going. But this is a tough, lifelong journey. At different stages we learn a little more and discover further direction, but for most of us it takes years of living through good and bad to find out who we are and where we're headed. At times we may think we have it cracked, but one door only leads to another, one piece of the jigsaw only reveals another part of a bigger picture.
Paul writes about our citizenship in the new kingdom. 'We are priests, kings, holy people,' he says in 1 Peter 2 v 9.
But that's not easy to grasp here in this world of sweat, flu, income tax, indigestion and in-laws.
In Ephesians 1 vv 3&4 Paul tells us that we've been given every spiritual blessing in the heavenly world. But here, in the earthly world, bad hair days and sleepless nights can often cloud the issue.

Before Jesus began his earthly ministry he heard from God. And it was the kind of message we'd all love to hear. The gospels tell us that, as he came up out of the water after his baptism, he heard a voice from heaven say: 'You are my own dear son, with whom I'm well pleased.'
In other words, 'That's my boy. You're brilliant. You can do it.'
We all need that kind of reassurance, don't we?

A friend of mine once said, 'Every girl needs to hear two things from her father. To know that she is beautiful, and to know that he loves her.'
We blokes don't like to admit it but we need it too, the knowledge that we're okay, we're acceptable, we have what it takes. We have nothing to prove.

Did Jesus hear an audible voice? Who knows? The people saw a dove descend on him and interpreted this as a sign of God's spirit. Matthew, Mark and Luke, who all record the event, probably weren't there on the day; only John, who had been one of John the Baptist's disciples before he transferred to following Jesus.
I've never heard a voice from the sky, my guess is you haven't either. We love to bandy round the phrases: 'God said this.' 'God told me that.' Often what we really mean is: 'I had a hunch.' 'A thought popped into my head.' And we have learnt to read these signs. Often God seems too subtle, too shy, for neon lights and voices in the sky.
So how are we to hear God say, 'You're mine, I'm pleased with you.'?
Where do we find that kind of affirmation? And how do we absorb it deep

inside, where it really matters? When we're yet again on a bad day, feeling cornered and insecure?

Questions:
1. Have you honestly ever heard God's voice? If so – how would you describe it?
2. Are there people affirm you?
3. What are spiritual blessings in heavenly places? What does that mean for you?
4. Maximus was driven by anger – what makes you angry? Are there positive results from your passion?
5. Did the clip make you think about anything else?

Title: Jesus Of Montreal – You Won't Like Me When I'm Angry

Themes: Jesus clears the temple; Passionate response and righteous anger

Bible refs: Matt 21 vv 12 & 13

Location of clip: 1 hour 3 mins 41 secs to 1 hour 7 mins 4 secs

Film Description:
A group of actors are staging a passion play for a local Catholic church. As they rehearse and then perform the Easter story for the tourists who pass by, their lives begin to mirror some of the events from the gospel stories.

Clip Description:
The girl playing Mary in the passion play has gone to an audition for a part in a new beer commercial. The actor playing Jesus accompanies her. The auditioning panel demand that she remove her sweater so they can see her figure, to see if it fits the role. However, the girl is not wearing a bra and refuses to expose herself for the leering executives also attending the audition. The panel press her and she is about to give in when Daniel (the actor playing Jesus in the passion play) stands and intervenes.
First he tells the actress she should not remove her top, then he lashes out at the panel for their desire to humiliate her. He turns over tables, sends a camera crashing to the floor and wrecks a computer monitor. Then, when one of the panel objects he walks up to her and slaps her across the face with a cable and subsequently chases the others from the auditorium.

Thoughts:
Daniel's reaction is truly shocking here. Truly shocking.
The situation is charged with embarrassment. The bullying panel are clearly intimidating the attractive actress and are intent on humiliating her in front of the businessmen.
Daniel arrives in the nick of time and rescues her from this difficult situation. But then he does not simply leave the building with her. Instead he smashes up expensive equipment and assaults another human being. Is this really necessary?

One of the difficulties for those of us who know the gospels well is really appreciating how subversive Jesus was. How counter-cultural.
He grew very angry indeed about the moneylenders in the temple. And no wonder. Forgiveness and relationship with God were at the heart of his message, yet here were businessmen and the religious elite turning it into a moneymaking scam. This was as far from the truth as you could get.

The father described in Jesus's prodigal son story is a truly shocking sight too. God can surely not be so naïve, so gullible as to race down a dirt track towards a filthy, stinking, greedy waster. Can he? God is omnipotent, omniscient, to be magnified and exalted and any other number of religious sounding words. Not according to Jesus. He hated anything that put God further away, hated anything that kept God and people apart. No wonder he got angry. What the moneylenders and religious authorities were doing was the equivalent of stepping between the prodigal and his father and saying, 'Sorry, dad, you can't give your wayward boy a welcome until he's paid us first. No money? Sorry mate, no hug.'

Jesus's description of God as an exuberant, excited parent is almost offensive to those who prefer to see God as a distant, cold Monarch, reigning on high.

John tells us that Jesus actually made a whip out of cords and used it to drive the animals out. That's premeditated. That's not a flash of anger, it takes time to make a whip.

Jesus burned with passion at times, and never more so than here. Thank goodness he did. If I had to pay good money every time I needed forgiveness I'd be in the red for the rest of my life.

Questions:
1. The moneylenders had taken the good laws of God and twisted them. Do we still do this today?
2. Have you ever felt angry about a situation that was just not right?
3. Would you have been embarrassed witnessing Jesus's outburst? Would it have shaken your faith in him?
4. What things in modern life would anger Jesus today?
5. Did the clip make you think about anything else?

Title: The Beach – Why Do All The Prodigals Run Away?

Theme: The Prodigal Son

Bible refs: Luke 15 vv 11-32

Location of clip: 33 secs to 2 mins 42 secs

Film Description:
Richard is bored with his life in America. He wants more, he wants to find another life, somewhere mysterious, somewhere strange. So he catches a flight to Thailand. While staying in a cheap hotel he is given a map of a secret island, an island so beautiful, so perfect it's beyond imagining. This is what he's been looking for, and so, with two new friends, he sets off in search of it.

Clip Description:
This is the opening credit sequence. Richard introduces himself, and introduces his quest for a better life.
'My name is Richard, so what else do you need to know? Stuff about my family or where I'm from – none of that matters. Not once you've crossed the ocean and cut yourself loose - looking for something more beautiful, something more exciting, and yes I admit – something more dangerous. So after eighteen hours in the back of an aeroplane… I finally touch down… in Bangkok. This is it. Good time city. The gateway to South-east Asia. Where dollars and deutschmarks get turned into counterfeit watches and genuine scars. This is where the hungry come to feed…'

Thoughts:
'This is where the hungry come to feed…' What is Richard hungry for? What are all those prodigals hungry for? I first encountered this movie when looking for something to illustrate the prodigal son story as told by Jesus in Luke's gospel chapter 15. I was surprised though. I thought it was a tale of boy leaves home, boy squanders his money on a decadent life, boy comes limping back.
But this is not the case here. Richard is certainly looking for a more exciting life, and yes it does involve soft drugs and alcohol. But it also centres around a community. A community of hungry people who gravitate together on a secluded island. This is not really about wild parties and anarchic behaviour. In fact the members of the island community are appalled when they return to the mainland and witness that kind of lifestyle. They are trying to build relationships, they work hard together, they're shaping a new kind of life for themselves.

Now I'm not saying that all the prodigals who ever ran away are in search of this kind of thing. But I do wonder whether there is actually something good, something healthy in their hunger for more. Often the prodigals want something real in life, something more extreme, something more meaningful, more engaging.

I once described myself as a prodigal considering running away again. Not from God, but certainly from the confines of church. Church can sometimes be a place of safety, a place of conformity, a place without extremes, a place where we can't shout, or say what we're really thinking. Genuine relationship involves energy, colour, life, argument, spontaneity and freedom of speech. Sadly these can be lacking in organised Christian gatherings. Niceness can squeeze out reality.

Yet when we look at Jesus, life seemed to be buzzing round him like fireflies around a campfire. He was often accused of being too happy, too lively, you won't find any mention in the gospels of people complaining that he was boring.

Questions:

1.   The older brother at the end of the story was angry about the outrageous, extravagant love demonstrated by his father. Have you ever felt annoyed by others who are different in your church?
2.   Are you aware of any prodigals in your life? Those hungry for more, but looking in damaging places?
3.   Have you ever found church gatherings to be dull? Have you ever been bored in church?
4.   What do you think Jesus would make of Richard's search for something more dangerous?
5.   Did the clip make you think about anything else?

Title: Braveheart – Blood And Guts

Theme: The crucifixion of Jesus

Bible refs: Luke 23 vv 26-42

Location of clip: 2 hours 30 mins 5 secs to 2 hours 33 mins 6 secs

Film Description: In 1820 Malcolm Wallace is killed fighting the troops of English King Edward Longshanks. His son William is deeply affected by the deaths of his father and his father's friends and, years later, when his new wife Morag is killed by English troops, Wallace begins to fight for the freedom of Scotland. However, after many battles and some successes he is captured by the English.

Clip Description:
William Wallace has been sentenced to death. He is to be hung, drawn and quartered. This is an appalling way to die, involving prolonged suffering and a slow, agonising death. What's more, he is to be a spectacle too. His death is paraded before the local people.
Two dwarves demonstrate what will happen to William as part of the warm up entertainment. Then William is brought out on the back of a cart, he is kneeling and his arms are tied to a cross, crucifixion-style. The crowd falls silent as the cart is led through them. Then one man fills his mouth with filthy spit and showers William with it. The crowd begin to shout and scoff, the people throw rotten fruit and vegetables. William flinches beneath the onslaught. When the cart reaches the stage at the front, William is led onto it by armed soldiers. He is taken to a table and shown the cruel weapons of torture that will slowly end his life. He stares at them. The executioner raises his hand and the crowd falls silent.

Thoughts:
When I first saw this part of the film my stomach turned. I felt sick and frightened. What on earth were they going to do to this man? The sight of the crowd baying for blood was hideous, their cruel taunting seemed cowardly and crass. As the instruments of torture were revealed I covered my face. This was not going to be easy viewing.
It made me realise how familiar I had become with the story of the crucifixion. I suddenly saw the whole thing again in a new light, the crowd baying for blood, the brutal soldiers, the cruel hours of torture, the prolonged slipping away of life.
As I watched the scene unfold and thought, 'What on earth are they going to do with this man?' it made me wonder - 'Is that what the disciples thought'? They did not know the end of the story. They did not know if the

Romans really had the power to kill Jesus. They expected victory, not cruel, bloody murder. They did not expect this at all. Did they watch with weak knees and churning stomachs and think, 'What on earth are they going to do with my friend?'

The power of a crowd is terrifying. I remember watching a documentary about the persecution of the Jews in World War II. The Nazi's encouraged crowds of locals to settle old scores and punish their neighbours. It was a horrible sight.

In Rwanda a million people died in just three months. How was that practically possible? Because crowds of local people were incited to hate their neighbours and wipe them out.

A crowd is so easily led. So easily manipulated.

The events surrounding the crucifixion must have been sickening and terrifying.

More recently Mel Gibson made The Passion – another movie which brings home the fact, that at the heart of Christianity, is a terrible, bloody murder. The murder of God himself.

Questions:

1. How do you find remembering the events of Easter each year? Has it made the story more powerful or too familiar?
2. We wear crosses in our ears and round our necks – has that changed our perception of the crucifixion?
3. Have you been part of a crowd – easily led for good or bad?
4. If you find this clip too hard to watch or think about – how does that make you feel? Pleased? Ashamed? Why?
5. Did the clip make you think about anything else?

Title: Chariots Of Fire – Fly, Run, Walk

Theme: Maturing in our faith

Bible refs: Isaiah 40 vv 21-31; Hebrews 6 vv 1&2

Location of clip: 1 hour 29 mins 40 secs to 1 hour 32 mins 10 secs

Film Description:
This is the account of two runners and their journeys of preparation and triumph in the 1924 Paris Olympics. Harold Abrahams, an English Jew who fought the system and won the gold medal in the 100 metres, and Eric Liddell, *the flying Scotsman*, who won the gold medal in the 400 metres. Two very different men with very different stories.

Clip Description:
As well as being an athlete Eric Liddell was also a preacher and an evangelist. Here he is in Paris, at the start of the Olympics, reading the lesson from Isaiah 40. His words are illustrated with images of athletes running, winning and losing. Originally Eric should have been running himself that day, in the heats for the 100metres, but he refused. He would not run on a Sunday because he felt it would dishonour God. So instead he is in church, reading the lesson, forfeiting his chance to be the fastest man on the planet.

Thoughts:
Paul uses the image of an athlete in his writings, it conjures up the sense of commitment, of dedication, of sacrifice, strength, perseverance and courage. These inspiring words from Isaiah, indeed any inspiring words from the Bible, only have power if they help us in our day-to-day living - on Monday morning when things are tough, humdrum, routine, tiring, frightening and demanding. When, like the athletes, we have sweat on our faces, mud on our clothes, blood on our knees, that's when the Bible can really spur us on to greatness. Jesus talks about the good things we do that only our heavenly father sees. The Living Bible says this: 'Your care for others is the measure of your greatness.' Greatness in God's eyes is often quiet, unseen, secret – but it all counts as greatness.

My understanding of this passage from Isaiah 40 has been revolutionised ever since reading a passage in Philip Yancey's book *Reaching for the Invisible God*.
Philip writes about the word order here.
'Those that wait upon the Lord… shall soar on wings like eagles, run and not grow weary, walk and not faint.'

The order seems wrong, surely you don't fly before you walk? Somewhere in my early days I got the idea that you improved as a Christian as life went by. First you walked, then you ran, then you soared. Yet that's not what Isaiah says.

I look back now on my early days as a Christian and realise that's when I did most of my soaring.

You couldn't shut me up about my faith. I worked in a bank and everyone in that branch knew I'd become a Christian. I was doing street evangelism, youth work, outreach events, missions. I was really flying.

Take a look at the Samaritan woman Jesus met in John chapter 4. She knew nothing about evangelism, she'd never read anything by Nicky Gumble – yet here she is bringing her whole village to Jesus. She's soaring up there. It seems to me that Christians are at their most contagious when they are first converted.

As time goes by the flying slows down, until we're walking with God. And that is the greatest challenge of all. In one sense it's easy when your faith is new and exciting and God seems to answer your every prayer. But God woos us on into maturity; he draws us into a relationship which has depth. He moves us from experiencing him as a heavenly provider to walking with him as a heavenly father. I'm inspired by the Old Testament heroes – when they prayed they haggled, wrestled, debated, and argued with God. Much of my prayer life has been *please, thanks* and *sorry*. God wants us to move on, to move away from the early days of seeing him just as a miracle worker. On into a solid relationship with real communication. A place where we have the nerve to trust God's love for us will not diminish, no matter how honest we are with him. He slows down so we can keep up with him.

Questions:

1. Did you begin your Christian life soaring on those eagle's wings? What stage are you at now?
2. Does maturity in faith mean leaving 'flying' behind?
3. Does it sadden you that there is this sense of slowing down, of needing to mature?
4. Do you find the thought of moving onto another level of relationship with God frightening in any way?
5. Have you had to do much wrestling in your journey with God?
6. Did the clip make you think about anything else?

Title: Liar, Liar – The Truth Will Set You Free

Theme: Honesty and integrity

Bible refs: John 8 vv 31 & 32

Location of clip: 36 mins 40 secs to 40 mins 12 secs

Film Description:
Fletcher Reede is a tough attorney. And an habitual liar. He lies for his job. Fletcher has a young son, Max, and when yet again Fletcher breaks a promise to be there on his birthday Max blows out the candles and makes a wish. He wishes that from now on his father will only be able to tell the truth. The wish comes true and Fletcher becomes a brutally honest man.

Clip Description:
Exhausted from his new-found honesty, Fletcher goes to meet Max at school. He bundles him out of his class and produces a cake and a candle. If Max wished his dad would stop lying then the solution is simple, he just has to unwish it. Fletcher lights the candle and Max shuts his eyes and blows it out. But the unwishing doesn't work. Max didn't really mean it. He wants his father to tell the truth, not to be a liar. Fletcher tries to argue his case.
'Everybody lies, mommy lies,' he says, and he explains that sometimes you just have to not tell the truth – because the truth is difficult to handle.

Thoughts:
'Everybody lies…' I guess we like to think that Christians always tell the truth, always come clean, never pass on slander, never embellish the truth. But of course that's ridiculous. We lie about all kinds of things. We often don't want to hurt people's feelings, we often want to blend in with the crowd, and we want an easy life. Telling the truth is not always popular, not always straightforward, and not always encouraging. It's a tough one, because we instinctively bend the facts or cloud the issues.

Take church meetings and home groups. How often do we sit there not understanding, or distracted, or disconnected from what is going on, yet afterwards commend those in charge for a meaningful time. When we have the chance to ask questions, share testimonies or request prayer, how often do we pick the acceptable options rather than the real stories from our lives. Whenever I'm asked for a prayer request I always filter out the nasty stuff and submit a pressing need for more of God's peace or direction in my life, (always a useful one) whereas what I probably need is more strength to resist sexual temptation, or the courage to put my beloved work aside and spend more time appreciating my family.

We follow a man who is *the truth* – yet often there can be more untruth inside the church than outside. We have bought into this idea that if we are Christians then we must surely all be sorted out, and not the muddled mess we all are. I love that definition of a Christian as *one beggar telling another where to find bread*. I think that's what I'll always be, a beggar in the spiritual gutter, scrabbling about for more of God's good bread. But dare we admit that? Dare we say that out loud?

Jesus said: 'The truth will set you free.' I have a hunch he wasn't meaning that if we go round quoting bits of the Bible out of context it will somehow make us superhuman... I reckon he meant that the kingdom of heaven is very present when people own up and start telling the truth about their mad, muddled lives.

Questions:
1. Do you think we really need to tell lies, or be economical with the truth in some situations?
2. Is God prompting you to be a little more honest about something?
3. Do you ever find yourself creating prayer requests in order to hide your real needs and issues?
4. How can we help each other be more honest with God and with one another?
5. Did the clip make you think about anything else?

Title: Shawshank Redemption – Only Took Six Years...

Theme: Perseverance

Bible refs: 1 Timothy 6 vv 11&12

Location of clips: 52 mins 30 secs to 55 mins; then 1 hour 3 mins 21 secs to 1 hour 7 mins 13 secs

Warning: These clips contain swearing.

Film Description:
Andy Dufresne is serving a life sentence in Shawshank prison for killing his wife and her lover. He claims he is innocent, but then so do all the other inmates. There isn't a guilty man in the prison. He befriends Red, an old hand who can get anything for anyone. Over their years together their friendship deepens and they survive many hardships together. Andy is a 'can do' kind of guy, he makes a difference to the prison. And though his early years are very grim and fraught with bullying and brutal intimidation, he survives and rises above this.

Clip Description:
Andy gets a job working in the prison library and decides to try and improve the selection of books there. He asks the Warden's permission to write to the authorities to ask for money to buy more books. The Warden agrees but tells him he knows already what they will say. Andy goes ahead and writes his letters anyway. He decides he will write one letter a week until he gets a response. The weeks roll by and Andy begins to do the income tax returns for the prison guards, in his former life he was an accountant. As time goes on he starts doing the returns for the guards from other prisons too. And still he writes those letters, week by week, and still he hears nothing back.
Then one day a collection of boxes arrives. They contain stacks of books for the library along with a cheque for $200 and a plea that he stop sending those letters.
Andy is overwhelmed. 'Only took six years,' he says, 'from now on I'll write two letters a week.'
To celebrate Andy puts on some opera and plays it over the prison tannoy system.

Thoughts:
Perseverance is key to the Christian life. No matter how many conferences you attend, no matter how many encouraging words you get, no matter how many good sermons or inspiring prayer times, you can still bet your

35

prayer book that you'll have many more days and weeks where nothing seems to be happening. I often hear the Bible described as *exciting* – well it is, I love it, but it's hard work to read. To find the exciting bits you have to dig away, read between the lines, do some background study, piece together the bits of the jigsaw. And that's the same for much of our Christian life. In one sense it's true to say being a Christian is the most exciting life you can have. But much of it is spent waiting, hoping, longing, believing, serving. What does Paul say? '…meanwhile, these three remain, faith, hope and love…' Faith and hope are certainly what we need in a world where the humdrum and the difficult often fill our nights and days.

Jesus spent three years chipping away at a handful of devoted people, then he saw them all scatter at the first sniff of trouble.
He prayed that all his followers might be one, a prayer he is still waiting to see answered.
Moses had to visit Pharaoh at least fifteen times to beg him to set the people free.
Ruth and Naomi lived lives of sadness and heartache with little of the biblical *excitement* we love to talk about.
Paul may have had an eventful last few years of journeying and shipwrecks and evangelism… But he spent years in the desert honing his faith and waiting for God to say, 'Go!'

Don't be deceived. For every person with an astonishing testimony, there are hundreds of thousands who wake up each morning, pray for their loved ones, then do the housework, or get on a cramped train, or sit in traffic, or try and sell something on the street.
For every fleeting moment of divine revelation, there may be six long years of waiting.

Questions:
1. Can you remember something you have given up waiting on God for?
2. Could you begin to ask him again?
3. Has there been a time when you persevered and it paid off?
4. Do you think there are times when we need to give in and stop persevering?
5. Did the clip make you think about anything else?

Title: Mission Impossible 2 – Mountain Top Experiences

Theme: Elijah and the Prophets of Baal

Bible refs: 1 Kings 18 & 19

Location of clip: 5 mins 32 secs to 8 mins

Film Description: Ethan Hunt is an agent with IMF (not to be confused with MFI) – Impossible Mission Force. Straight out of the 007 mode, this is a man who will attempt anything. He has faced death on many occasions and will clearly do so again. Ethan is a witty, intelligent, multi-talented action man – with good looks and charm in spades. Some people have all the luck…

Clip Description:
This is the opening credit sequence in which Ethan Hunt climbs a mountain on holiday and yet still can't get away from his day job! Ethan climbs with no ropes or equipment, he's quite clearly been to the James Bond school of mountaineering. At one point he jumps, slips and hovers, one hand clasping a rock, but then he summons his strength and pulls himself up. Climbing takes a while, but when he reaches the top it's worth the thrills and spills, the view is awesome.

Thoughts:
A friend of mine once said, 'The great thing about mountain tops is that you get perspective, you see things more clearly, you see where you've come from, you see the bigger picture. (As long as it's not cloudy!)'
We can make the mistake of thinking the Bible is a book of mountain top experiences, and as a result we are disappointed when our lives do not mirror this assumption. But in reality the Bible is about real people, struggling to get from one mountain to another. Most of the time is spent climbing and descending, falling and slipping. Every single Old Testament hero had to wait and struggle.
Elijah experienced the ultimate mountain top experience, he shows us the ultimate contest: what would really happen when the living God went head to head with all the other false gods. Would he come through? Would he stay silent?
Well, God came through, and big time. On Mount Carmel he silenced the prophets of Baal and showed them beyond all doubt who had the power. Was Elijah elated? Was there a religious revival? No. Within a short space of time Elijah was on the run, his life was falling apart, and there was no renewed surge of faith in the land. Elijah was a disappointed man, very much broken by his mountain top experience. He ended up in the desert,

hiding. But it turned out to be a good place to discover that God cares more about relationships than power. God has all the power already – it's the relationships that he's still out there looking for.

In the desert Elijah hears the now famous *still, small voice* and for a long time I thought that was very much about the way God speaks to us. In the stillness and in the quiet. But now I think differently. I often hear God in the bustle, in the city, in the busy places. In the Bible there are certainly times when we are encouraged to be still and listen, but there are times when people hear God in the normal noise of life.

There's a great little poem in Martin Wroe's book *When You Haven't Got a Prayer*. It's called *Noise* and contains the line,

'I am not tranquil except when I am asleep... So, what's the chance of a still big voice in the noise...?'

God speaks to Elijah in a small voice, but look at the context, **Elijah's already having a conversation with God.** The still small voice occurs in the middle of a dialogue. Elijah doesn't have to strain to hear it. So what's the point of this?

God shows Elijah a powerful hurricane, it tears rocks from mountains it's so strong. Bear in mind the fact that Elijah has just witnessed an incredible display of God's power. What he's probably thinking is – if only we had more of that, then people would really repent. Next there's an earthquake, uprooting bits of the planet in its wake. And then there's a huge fire, scorching heat destroying all in its path. Frightening, powerful imagery – yet it's as if God says a startling thing, 'I'm not in all that. I want you to listen out for my voice, it's a different, unique thing. Know me better Elijah, I'm not really about power – I'm about relationship.'

Questions:

1. Can you recall surprising moments when God has spoken to you? Perhaps through others doing something, or saying something? Or an event that took place?
2. It's so tempting to live with the notion that we should be seeing more of God's power. How can we help one another cope with the mundane nature of life?
3. Have you had many mountaintop experiences? Have they helped you long-term?
4. Does God speak to you in a still small voice? Do you ever hear him in the noise and bustle?
5. Did the clip make you think about anything else?

Title: Jerry Maguire – Things We Think And Do Not Say

Theme: What inspires you? What burns away inside you?

Bible refs: Joel 2 vv 28 & 29; 2 Timothy 1 vv 5-7

Location of clip: 5 mins 35 secs to 7 mins 47 secs

Warning: This clip contains swearing

Film Description:
Jerry Maguire is a sports agent. His aim in life is to make as much money as possible from as many clients as possible. But Jerry has lost his way. Money has become his god, and everything else revolves around this. He has lost sight of the people he is serving.

Clip Description:
One night Jerry Maguire has an epiphany. He cannot sleep and his brain begins working overtime. Suddenly he sees things afresh, sees things as he used to see them. He remembers the words of the man who inspired him, the late great Dickie Fox: 'The key to this job is personal relationships.'
In the middle of the night he begins writing a mission statement. He writes twenty-five pages of suggestions for the future of the company he works for. 'Suddenly,' he says, 'I was my father's son again,' recalling the simple pleasure of his job. The reasons he became an agent in the first place. He says, 'It was the me I always wanted to be.'
He takes what he's written and makes 110 copies which he then distributes to everyone in the company. He calls it *The things we think and do not say*. It is a work of inspiration. Everyone is impressed. Ultimately it gets him fired.

Thoughts:
The things we think and do not say... How different might the kingdom of God be if we spoke out some of those things. Conformity and politeness can be good and useful things, but often they quench passion and purpose and result merely in frustration and mediocrity. Jesus spoke out the things he thought, he confronted injustice and silly religiosity.
He squared up to leaders who put burdens on their congregations, he squared up to politicians who were corrupt and hypocritical. He scooped up the downtrodden and the young and lifted them above other people. He told stories that were subversive, violent, shocking, funny and difficult. He went off for times of quiet with his father and his head must have been

buzzing with ideas whenever he came back. Sometimes it's after time spent with his father that a new development takes place.

At the last supper Jesus tells his disciples; 'When everything is ready, I will come and get you, so that you will always be with me where I am. And you know where I am going and how to get there.'

All the other disciples sit there nodding sagely, it's only good old honest Thomas who has the guts to say: 'No, we don't know, Lord, we haven't any idea where you are going, so how can we know the way?'

Good old Thomas, he doesn't just sit there pretending it's all okay - he speaks out.

When were you last inspired? Have you had moments when God reminded you why you're alive, why you're following him? Admittedly it's frightening, speak out and in the daylight people may pat you on the back, but in the dark they may stab you in the same place.

It's said that 10 per cent of any congregation do 90 per cent of the work. Don't the other 90 per cent ever get inspired? What are you thinking right now, that you'd rather not say?

Wake up! Write it down, speak it out, do something about it, but whatever you do… Don't just sit on it till it goes away and you've become old and stale and frustrated.

Questions:
1. Are you part of the 90 per cent or part of the 10 per cent? Be honest now. What might happen if the 10 per cent took a break?
2. If you are inspired and bursting to do something – can you find avenues to explore this?
3. Any changes take a long time, it's not easy to stay in for the long haul. What do you think of that?
4. There may be a cost… Jerry Maguire lost his job. Have you considered this?
5. Did the clip make you think about anything else?

Title: Love Actually – Secret Angels

Theme: God is at work out there in the world every hour of every day

Bible refs: Hebrews 13 vv 1&2

Location of clip: 1 hour 12 mins 50 secs to 1 hour 17 mins 30 secs

Film Description:
Love Actually is a collection of love stories, some are just bright fluffy fairy tales, others deal with the grittier side of loving - infidelity in marriage, sacrificing a lover because of needy family members, the long-term development of a relationship compared to casual sex.

Clip Description:
Harry has a secretary. Her name is Mia and she has a crush on him the size of Ecuador. What's more – she's not afraid to let him know. Just one problem. Harry is married to Karen. Christmas is coming and Harry and Karen go out for a spot of Christmas shopping for the in-laws. On his way out of the office Harry stops to talk to Mia, who asks him to buy a present for her. Harry is thrown by this, but begins to entertain the idea. In a large department store Karen goes off looking for presents. Harry is left to his own devices and spots a nearby jewellery counter. He has five minutes, will it be long enough to buy Mia a special something?

The male assistant disappears as he approaches and a new one steps in his place, almost from nowhere. Harry quickly selects a necklace. It is £300 – he'll take it. Would sir like it wrapped? Okay then. The assistant then begins a convoluted and prolonged process involving cinnamon sticks, holly, plastic bags, festive greenery and a huge box. Much to Harry's protestations. (You really have to watch this to get the best from it.) In the end Harry runs out of time and hastily backs away from the counter as Karen reappears. He is safe, but he has no present for Mia.

Thoughts:
I had a sneaking suspicion that the shop assistant in this scene was really an angel, and on buying the DVD I discovered I was right. There's a big clue (the size of Ecuador) in one of the deleted scenes. If you or I wandered down a busy street and saw a small child run out into the road – we would rescue it. Of that there's no doubt. It would not matter that we didn't know them – we would instinctively want to save them from harm. So it is with God. He is at work out there constantly, rescuing people from harm, calling them back from danger – and in this case – attempting to prevent Harry from damaging his marriage.

41

God has a great sense of humour, so it does not surprise me to find there are times when he distracts us from danger and trouble with a wry smile and a dry wit. Angels don't always appear with a big sword and a stern expression, as with say, Balaam, in the book of Judges. Sometimes humour is a great way to diffuse temptation. Sometimes a kind word and the smile of God are just what we need to keep us from harm.

However, I am also very aware of the millions of situations when there is no rescue. When trouble comes and damage happens. I have no answers for this. In the end Harry still buys the necklace, he returns to the store, presumably on a day when the angel is not around, and he purchases the necklace which breaks his wife's heart and causes a whole lot of trouble.

Maybe sometimes we don't recognise the angels when they turn up, maybe sometimes we ignore them, maybe sometimes they try but cannot break through to help. Maybe we'll just never know. All I can say is that I'm grateful for the times in my life when angels have changed things for me.

Questions:
1. Have you, or anyone you know, ever seen an angel?
2. Have you had some other kind of experience of God's intervention?
3. Has another person ever been an 'angel' to you?
4. In Hebrews 13 v 2, the writer encourages us to show hospitality to strangers, for some people who have done this have entertained angels without realising it. Have you ever wondered about this?
5. Did the clip make you think about anything else?

Title: Regarding Henry – What Are Your Bad Knees?

Theme: God can use our weaknesses

Bible refs: 1 Corinthians 12 vv 6-9; 1 Corinthians 1 vv 21-25

Location of clip: 1 hour 21 mins 5 secs to 1 hour 25 mins 20 secs

Warning: This clip contains swearing

Film Description:
Henry is a hard-nosed lawyer. Brilliant at his job and hard on his family. Then one day he is caught up in a robbery in a store. He gets caught in the crossfire and ends up with a bullet in the head and the spine. As a result he has to learn to walk and talk again, and his personality is a whole lot more playful, more humble. Sounds like a dream doesn't it? Just one problem – he no longer fits into his life as the tough lawyer. After rehabilitation he returns to work, but he doesn't fit in anymore, he's not the same man.

Clip Description:
As a result of this he has a breakdown. He lies in bed unwilling to face the world. Things make no sense to him anymore. He doesn't want to carry on. So his wife calls Bradley. Bradley is the nurse who taught Henry to walk and talk again. He became a good friend and could be the man to revive Henry's flagging spirits.
They sit at the kitchen table drinking beer and Henry tells Bradley his troubles. Bradley listens, nods wisely then says, 'I got bad knees.'
Henry is perplexed.
'I got bad knees,' he says again, 'got 'em playing college football.'
Bradley used to be a brilliant player, until the day he caught a ball and his knees popped. The nurse who taught him to walk again was so cool that Bradley decided that's what he wanted to be. He says to Henry, 'Now ask me if I mind having bad knees.' And before Henry can ask he says, 'No... if it wasn't for my knees I'd never have met you.'

Thoughts:
'If it wasn't for my knees I would never have met you – so I don't mind having bad knees, no.' Paul wrote in Corinthians – 'God's power is made perfect, or works best, in our weakness.' I so wish that wasn't the case. If you are like me, you probably want to hide your weaknesses, they're embarrassing. But God seems to say to me – those are the bits I want to use – those bits you despise – those bits you regret and hate about yourself – those are the very tools you have for changing the world in

43

some way. Some people will be spectacularly successful in life. All of us will, at some point, be broken. Our bodies, our minds, our spirits, our hearts. One way or another we will be battered by life. It's a shared experience, a shared language – and if we take the Bible seriously – it seems to be the currency God uses in this world.

Jesus did an amazingly powerful miracle when he fed probably 20,000 people with five loaves and two fish. Yet this powerful thing did not result in revival, in fact, people turned away in their droves when Jesus would not go on doing the magic for them. Instead, it was when Jesus was weak, bloody and naked, stretched out like so much raw meat on a cross of wood, that's when he did his finest work. In that terrible, broken state, in that very unspiritual of places, in those abhorrent, despicable hours, that's when he saved the planet.

Could that really be God's work? That convicted criminal seeping blood and bodily fluids up there next to those foul-mouthed terrorists? Apparently so.

I have no idea what your bad knees are, but my guess is, if you offer them to the one who understands the power of weakness, he will find a way to use them to help someone.

Questions:
1. Most of us pray that God will heal or take away their weaknesses – even Paul did that – what do you think of the notion that God may want to combine them with your strengths in some way?
2. What do you consider to be your weaknesses?
3. What do you think about the notion of making yourself vulnerable in front of others?
4. Have you ever offered your weaknesses to God for him to use?
5. Did the clip make you think about anything else?

Title: The Mission – I Want To Break Free

Theme: Freedom

Bible refs: Galatians 4 vv 1-12; Psalm 103 vv 8-17

Location of clip: 28 mins to 40 mins 10 secs

Film Description:
Mendoza is a slave trader in South America. He journeys into the jungles to find the local tribes so he can take them by force and sell them into slavery. One day Mendoza kills his brother in a duel over a woman they both love. He is racked by guilt, remorse and self-pity. He feels there is no redemption for him. No way out.

Clip Description:
Gabriel is a brother in the local Jesuit community. He knows what Mendoza has done so he comes to see him and offer him hope. Mendoza says there is no hope but Gabriel knows better. He offers Mendoza a way back to life. Mendoza begrudgingly accepts.
Mendoza bundles his heavy armour and weaponry into a large net. He then ties this to his back and drags it through the jungle, across rivers and up steep cliff faces, back towards the native tribes he has wronged. The journey is hard and very long. At one point one of the Jesuits takes pity on Mendoza and cuts him free from his heavy burden, but the time is not right, Mendoza is not ready to be free, and the Jesuit is not the right person to do the job. Mendoza chases the burden and ties it back to himself. On he goes, the Jesuit brothers alongside him, dragging this weight through mud and rain and dirt.

Finally he reaches the jungle village of one of the local tribes. The home of the people he has been kidnapping and selling into slavery. There is a tense moment as they realise it is Mendoza and one of the men comes running with a knife. For a second he holds it to Mendoza's throat. Perhaps this is what Mendoza wants, freedom from his life, freedom from having to live with what he's done.
But no. The native laughs, turns the knife and uses it to cut the burden from Mendoza's back. He pushes it to the cliff edge and rolls it away, beyond reach, into the waters far below. Mendoza breaks down, and the Jesuits and the natives laugh and cry along with him.

Thoughts:
This is an incredibly effective portrayal of release from the past. Mendoza is haunted by his mistake, hounded by the crime he has committed.

It takes courage for Mendoza to take the challenge Gabriel offers him. He does of course, and we see him drag the tools of his wretched trade all the way up the side of a mountain, through unforgiving forests and across raging rivers. He drags this burden and won't let it go. When others try and cut him free he fights them off. It is only when he meets those with the power to free him, in this case the indigenous people he has enslaved, only then is the freedom real, and his life begins again amidst joy and tears. We can drag the burdens around for years, and it's only when we're ready to be cut free – that we will find release. And only from the one with the power to do the cutting. By bundling up his armour and hauling it up a mountain Mendoza was able to face up to his guilt and the burden of it. Our perception of sin is distorted of course. Mendoza was involved in a whole lifestyle of sin before he ever killed his brother, but he felt no guilt, no remorse about kidnapping innocent people and selling them into slavery.

Freedom is a topic often preached about and sung about in Christian circles. But what does it mean? Fundamentally, Jesus has freed us from the ultimate effects of death and rebellion. The fall of Eden has been reversed. As psalm 103 says: 'God does not punish us as we deserve...' I find that such a heartening verse, especially when I frequently condemn myself. In fact, forgiving myself is really the issue; God has already taken the decision to forgive me wholeheartedly and warmly. But this refers to an invisible world, almost an invisible freedom. What about the visible world? What about the here and now?
The freedom to fail. The freedom to cry. The freedom to hope in a brighter future. The freedom to walk with God through every situation the world throws at us. I guess what we're not so free from is the power of temptation and the power of recurring sins, e.g. gossiping, criticising, thinking bad thoughts, grappling with sexual temptation. These are real things that we all must face on a daily basis. Yes, we are free from the ultimate power of them – but we still live very much in the real world, and we can be realistic about this. What do you think?

Questions:
1. Sometimes good things can hold us back too – times in the past when we had great faith and experienced moments of real growth. Sometimes we can hanker to be back then, instead of continuing to grow as people and keep moving forward. What do you think?
2. Can you identify burdens you are carrying around?
3. Do you think we are too hard on ourselves regarding the burdens we must face each day?
4. How can we best help one another with the burdens we drag around, bearing in mind the fact that we cannot force each other to break free?
5. Did the clip make you think about anything else?

Title: Patch Adams – It's The Way You Tell 'Em

Theme: The healing power of humour

Bible refs: Jeremiah 33 vv 10&11; Genesis 21 vv 4-7

Location of clip: 26 mins 30 secs to 29 mins 55 secs

Film Description:
Patch Adams has a breakdown, and as a result checks into a mental health clinic. There he observes poor practise demonstrated by the doctors. So he checks himself out, newly inspired to start again and train to be a doctor. However Patch has a wicked sense of humour, and he can't help but bring this into his days whilst training. He frequently gets into trouble with his teachers and superiors because he will not play by the rules. He believes that humour can help heal people.

Clip Description:
Patch has a placement in a hospital, but gets into trouble one day for messing about. When he sees a senior doctor heading his way he hides in a nearby ward to escape punishment. When the doctor has passed and Patch turns to see where he is, he finds himself in a rather subdued children's ward. He goes up to the sick children one by one and starts to make them laugh, putting on silly voices and funny noses and generally throwing himself around. Slowly, bit by bit, the sombre ward comes to life. Children sit up and take notice and the room is soon filled with the sound of excited giggling quickly followed by unrestrained laughter.
Patch has just placed a couple of bedpans on his feet and is dancing like a clown when the door bursts open and in steps a severe-looking nurse, come to see what all the noise is about. Patch grins sheepishly, sneaks past her and quickly leaves, stopping just long enough to peep back in through the window and wave at the children.

Thoughts:
Humour's a funny thing – especially in religious circles. Though it's clear to most of us how healthy and affirming it can be to have a jolly good laugh, when it comes to God we suddenly feel the need to be awfully serious. It's almost as if we don't quite believe that God created funny things in the first place. Somehow holiness has been confused with seriousness.
I can't help thinking myself that humour has to be one of the holiest things on the planet. It's so powerful, so life-affirming, so releasing. It often brings balance, perspective, reality. It can diffuse tension, grief and super-spirituality. I remember someone once telling me of an occasion in a church service when the leader was mightily pushing everyone to sing a

particular song with great gusto. The song was called: 'As the deer pants for the water…' and the leader was assuring the congregation that 'God really wants your pants.' Great stuff! If they didn't have a laugh about it I bet God did.

We take life so seriously don't we? And religion even more so. There are very few Islamic comedians. I doubt if the Jehovah's Witnesses tell knock, knock jokes… But maybe they should!

Surely this is one of the tricks of the devil. To make life with God look so dull, so sombre, so lifeless, so drab. I can't really imagine all those children and prostitutes and crooks and hardened fisherman looking all righteous and pompous as they hung around Jesus and heard his wisecracks and his jokes. The Pharisees accused them all of having much too much of a good time. Jesus couldn't possibly be from God – people were laughing far too much!

Okay – so humour can be misused, of course it can – but so can anything. No one would argue that God didn't make a particular tree just because someone cut it down and made cruel whips from the wood. Anything can be misused by people. Even the Bible.

Questions:
1. Much of humour is cultural, which is why it's difficult to spot the jokes in the Bible. Can you think of any humour you have spotted in the Old or New Testament?
2. What do you think about the suggestion that church is too serious?
3. Think of someone you know who is full of life and good humour – isn't that something of what Jesus must have been like? After all, he came to bring fullness of life.
4. Can you think of any times when you have seen humour help people?
5. Did the clip make you think about anything else?

Title: Romeo & Juliet – New Words For An Old Message

Theme: Communicating the Bible in a relevant way

Bible refs: Matthew 13 vv 34 & 35;

Location of clip: 23 secs to 3 mins 24 secs

Film Description:
This is the beginning of Shakespeare's *Romeo and Juliet* – but told as never before. Some of the text has been removed and replaced with fast moving visual imagery. The characters are contemporary and dressed in modern costume. The language is still Shakespearean and the story remains intact, but the music and cinematography have turned this into a tale for the 21st century.
The plot in 9 words: two unlucky lovers, two feuding families, two sad suicides.

Clip Description:
The voice-over from the beginning of Romeo and Juliet is accompanied by images of televisions, advertising billboards, modern cities, traffic, newspaper headlines and violence. A newsreader introduces the story, reading to us from a portable TV set. A voice-over takes over, again delivering the introductory lines, this time accompanied by snapshots of the characters, in newspaper articles and action stills, character names appear like bullet-points on the screen. The action moves to a petrol station as the rival gangs of the Montague and Capulet Boys arrive in cool cars and confront each other. Their swords are now handguns, and the ensuing battle includes gunfire, ricocheting bullets and exploding petrol tanks.

Thoughts:
This is Shakespeare as we've not seen it before.
The story is still faithfully delivered but the media has changed dramatically.
When it ran in cinemas this version played to packed audiences of teenagers for weeks.
A new set of images for a classic tale. Director Baz Lurhman takes the old, old story of *Romeo and Juliet* and makes it accessible and meaningful for teenagers and young men.
One of the great challenges today is how we tell the precious Bible stories in ways that make sense and resonate with people now. This is nothing new – Jesus looked for new ways to tell his message to a generation that had completely the wrong idea about God.

The Bible is seen by many as old, dusty and difficult to read. Let's face it. It's difficult to read even if you're a Christian. We have to do all we can to get that message out there. We have to move away from simply reading it aloud in that slightly strange, rather serious voice we reserve for Sunday services. When the stories in the Bible actually took place they were events full of real people, experiencing real life. We rob it of its power and relevance if we are too precious about it and only tell it in ways that are frankly outdated and dull.

God's word is living and active, full of wisdom and wonder. But to get at the truth behind the words we have to work harder, dig deeper, and then tell it like it's never been told before. Jesus only told stories about farmers and fishing because that resonated with his audience. David wrote the 23rd psalm the way he did because he had been a shepherd. These were contemporary images when they were first delivered.

God moves on. He won't stand still. I love the image in Exodus of the two pillars leading the Israelites on their journey to the Promised Land – the pillar of cloud by day and the pillar of fire by night. The pillars were unpredictable, you could never say when or for how long they would keep moving. But keep moving they did. And God is the same today, he keeps moving forward. Let's not imagine that the images and words used to communicate him are inherently holy in themselves – they are just the vehicle. It's the message about God and his nature that is holy. How can we pass that message on in an age when Samaritans are no long bad guys and the only lambs most of us ever see are cling-filmed in Styrofoam trays?

Questions:
1. Do you think you put on a different voice when you read the Bible or pray aloud in church? Feel free to be honest now!
2. Some people say the Bible is so important we must not change it in any way – others would argue that it's so important we must find ways to re-interpret it for today's people. What do you think?
3. What impacts you? Do you have a version of the Bible that helps you connect with the message?
4. How can we help those who cannot read, those who are dyslexic, those who just don't like books?
5. Did the clip make you think about anything else?

Title: The Truman Show – Who's In Charge Here?

Theme: Is God in control?

Bible refs: Genesis 1 vv 26-30

Location of clip: 58 min 48 secs to 1 hour 3 min 33 secs

Film Description:

Truman Burbank lives in a television show. He just doesn't know it. He was born there and his whole life has been on the small screen. Millions of viewers tune in every day to watch his existence unfold. Everyone else in the show is an actor, and his home is one big film set. The show was created by Christof – the man who has ultimate control over Truman's life. He can bring on the sun, or send the rain. He directs the other characters, feeds them lines and controls their destinies.

Clip Description:

We see an advert for the show, a résumé of the story so far. Then we meet Christof the creator. He explains about Truman's life, about the times people have tried to break into the show unscripted, about the life Truman lives.

Thoughts:

At the start of the film Marlon, Truman's on-screen best friend, says to the audience: 'It's all true, nothing you see on the show is fake, it's just…controlled.'
What does it mean for someone to be in control? It's something many Christians often proclaim. 'God is in control.'
Is he moving us around like pawns? Does he treat us like Christof treats Truman, manipulating our moves and the moves of those people around us?
If that's the case what is the gift of freewill all about? What did it mean for God to hand over to Adam and Eve the gift of choice.
'You may eat the fruit of any tree in the garden, except the fruit of the tree which gives knowledge of good and evil…'
God gives the clear guidance, but the tree is still left within their reach. It's their decision whether to eat or not.

Christof is not an attractive character, though he says he cares for Truman, he is actually impulsive, selfish and manipulative. Most of us would say we all know God is not like that, but interestingly enough, we all have days when we fear God might be.
Jesus told a parable about a persistent widow and an unjust judge. It's

often viewed as a parable about prayer, and I'm sure it is, but I think it's also a parable about our view of God. Why did Jesus liken God to an unjust judge? Surely that's not theologically correct?

I believe he was tapping into the image of God many of his hearers had tucked away in their heads.
We're no different. We all have times when we think God is being unjust and days when we fear he will judge us. One of Jesus's biggest challenges was to show people God was not like that at all. It's probably the biggest misconception of God ever. And it's still so popular today.

Questions:
1. Have you ever considered the possibility that your personal choices, your tastes, desires and passions are important to God? That he wants you to be free to choose?
2. Why is it so important to feel that God is *in control*? And what does that mean?
3. Good role models and parental figures can help us see God as the kind, caring father he is. Can you think of good examples of this in your own life – friends or family members?
4. What can we do on those days, in those moments, when we fear God's judgement, when we find it hard to see his compassion and forgiveness?
5. Did the clip make you think about anything else?

Title: Schindler's List – Loving The Hard Way

Theme: Compassion and courage

Bible refs: Matthew 25 vv 31-46

Location of clip: 2 hours 1 min 40 secs to 2 hours 4 mins 50 secs

Film Description:
Oskar Schindler, a German businessman, saved the lives of twelve hundred Polish Jews during World War II. As the Nazi forces cracked down on the Polish Jews, Schindler built a factory and employed them to make pots and pans for the war effort. When their ghetto was dissolved he built his own concentration camp where they were treated fairly and when the camp was closed and other Jews moved to Aushwitz, Schindler had his own workers moved to Czechoslovakia.

Clip Description:
A trainload of Jews stands in Krakow station, ready to ship the people to Aushwitz. A group of soldiers sits on the platform laughing and drinking. Oskar Schindler arrives and greets the superior officer, Amon Goet. Schindler asks for some water and then watches impassively as the Jews continue to be herded onto the train.
The day is hot, very hot. And these poor people have nothing to drink. Oskar spots a nearby fire hydrant and suggests they get a hose and hose down the train. The Germans laugh about it and he laughs with them, but he still gets his own way and the bemused soldiers watch as he oversees the wanton spraying of the overheated carriages.
When he discovers that the hose will not stretch the full length of the train, Oskar suggests that he bring some extra from his factory. Once again the soldiers joke about this, but once again he gets his own way. As the scene ends we see him bribing the guards with a crate of wine. Telling them to pass out water during the train ride.

Thoughts:
'This is cruel Oskar, you're giving them hope!' So says Amon Goet. Indeed he is, just the kind of hope Jesus encouraged us to hand out regularly and extravagantly. What good will a little spray of water do for people who are on their way to the gas chambers? Presumably the same good that giving out a cup of water to a street beggar will do. We are not asked to work it all out. We are simply asked to be kind. We are asked to show compassion. We're not building an empire here, we're just littering the world with rampant acts of caring.
Love is such an overused word – I shy away from it in this context – love

53

can mean anything these days.
What Schindler demonstrates here is intelligent, cunning, witty compassion.

And it's worth noting that Oskar is very good-natured about his benevolence.
When he suggests using the fire hose and one of the soldiers says, 'Where's the fire?' he laughs along with the rest of them.
No false piety here. He's one of the lads. But by joining in with their jibes he is softening them up, preparing the way for him to win through.

But this kind of stuff takes courage. There's a saying, *for evil to prosper all that is necessary is for good people to do nothing.*
Following this you could also say, *for unkindness to flourish all that's required is for kind people to bow to peer pressure.* It's embarrassing to show an interest in people in public. It's easier to bury our heads in our books and newspapers. I should know, I've done it a million times on tubes and buses.

Questions:

1. Sometimes we hold back from helping people because we fear it may be dangerous, or we may be misunderstood. Have you experienced this?
2. How can we bring hope to the people we know who need it, even temporarily?
3. It's often the little things that matter. A smile here and there, a kind word, a listening ear. Would you feel able to offer these in the course of your day?
4. How can we remind ourselves about these things in the rush and pressure of busy days?
5. Did the clip make you think about anything else?

Title: Hugo – A Shared Language

Theme: Weakness

Bible refs: 2 Corinthians 12 vv 6-10

Film Description:

Martin Scorsese is famous for brutal movies such as *Goodfellas, The Departed, Raging Bull* and *Gangs of New York*. The kind of films that contain violence, swearing and complex, hard-bitten characters - shocking but honest stuff. So a heart-warming family film from the master of the mean streets is a very different kind of shock to the system.

Hugo is a heartbroken orphan who lives in a railway station, secretly maintaining the clocks there and pilfering food to survive. His late father taught him the ways of all things clockwork and he loves building and rebuilding toys and gadgets. He 'borrows' bits of machinery from a local toyshop owner, and eventually this brings him a whole world of trouble and discovery. This is a movie chock full of weird and wonderful characters who spend time in the station, all of them damaged in some way.
It's not quite like any family movie I've seen before, dealing with loneliness and heartache and disappointment alongside the wonder and magic of movie-making and storytelling.

Clip Description:

There is a wonderful moment in this film when Hugo tells his new friend Isabelle something his father once taught him. 'Clockwork toys do not come with spare parts,' he says, 'and the world is like that too. It does not come with spare parts.' So no one is a spare part, everyone is important, here to play their unique part.

Sacha Baron Cohen plays an awkward station master who is secretly in love with flower seller Lisette. He has been injured in the First World War and now wears a leg brace which keeps locking at inopportune moments, highlighting his disability. One day this happens whilst he is in conversation with Lisette and embarrassed he turns to flee from her, but as he goes he blurts out about his leg being damaged in the war and not fixable. Lisette quickly replies that she lost her brother in the same war. Suddenly they are united by a common thread, the war has left them both with loss.

Thoughts:

This is one of those moments I'll remember. Weakness is a shared language, more so than success. Everyone has weakness in their life, we can all speak the lingo. A couple of years ago I went with some friends to hear Rob Bell speak, we drove an eight hour round trip for a two hour gig but it was well worth it. At one point he asked us to write 'I know how you feel' in our non-writing hand on a piece of card. Then he asked those of us whose lives had been touched by cancer in any way to stand and hand our cards to one another. We gently passed over our poorly scribbled messages to each other. Then he asked those whose lives had been touched by debt to do the same. Rob made the point that had he asked us to stand if we had visited Spain for a holiday it would not have had the same meaning at all.

Weakness is so hard to voice. Money troubles, sickness, relationship problems, past embarrassments - these are so, so hard to share, and sometimes all we can do, like Sacha Baron Cohen's station master, is hurriedly run for cover whilst blurting out the truth. But the unique thing about Christianity is that we can always look to that cross, where we find God writing with his weak hand, saying, 'I know all about weakness and embarrassment and loss and poverty.'

What do you think?

Questions:
1. Do you feel able to discuss this issue, or is it too sensitive?
2. We often want to hold up Jesus as a powerful kind of Superman, perhaps we should talk more of his normality and vulnerability. What do you think?
3. There are lots more weak, poor Christians in the world than rich, powerful ones, how do you feel about that? Did you realise you are part of a small majority?
4. Have you had moments when you have risked blurting out the truth about your weaknesses and/or mistakes? What was the result?
5. Did the clip make you think about anything else?

Title: Austin Powers, International Man of Mystery – Let's Talk About Sex

Theme: er… sex

Bible refs: Song of Songs 1 vv 1-16

Location of clip: 22 mins 32 sex to 25 mins 8 sex; OR (for a less extreme clip) 1 min 29 sex to 3 mins 53 sex

Film Description:
Austin Powers is a spoof of James Bond with a huge ham fist of *Carry On* humour thrown in for good measure. The plot doesn't really matter too much in this instance – it's just liberally sprinkled with jokes about sex.

Clip Description:
In the first clip Austin and Vanessa are aboard Austin's private jet. Vanessa wants to focus on the mission in hand – trying to track down the evil Dr Evil. But Austin has been cryogenically frozen for 30 years and would rather focus on sex.
The second clip is the credit sequence. Austin and a whole troop of dancers come leaping down the streets of sixties London like something out of a Cliff Richard movie. There's very little direct reference to sex in this clip, but if you are concerned about offending anyone it's the safer of the two extracts.

Thoughts:
Two things are for sure.
1. The world won't stop talking about sex.
2. The church won't start.
So what are we to do? I guess the dear old Victorians started it, they were obsessed with death and in denial about sex. And as many of our church gatherings are still firmly rooted in the Victorian way of things we've inherited a deep sense of shame and embarrassment to do with any activity in the underwear department.

This is a difficult issue to discuss, especially in mixed groups (male and female) but if we don't address it, it just festers away and comes out in all the wrong places.
Sex is a massive issue for most men (I'm afraid I can't comment regarding women)… But I often wonder at the fact that we have a multitude of sermons on just a few spiritual issues, but very few sermons on this – a vital life issue. Let's face it, we're all sexual beings – yet walk into any church meeting and you'd think we'd had our libidos surgically removed on our day of conversion.

We pretty much know the right answers to the difficult questions – but that doesn't mean it helps us cope with all our struggling and failing and picking ourselves up again. How many of us attend church under a cloud because yet again we lost our footing and fell into the same old sexual bad habit. And the worst thing we can do is assume that we're in it alone.

Believe me, everyone else in the room you're in now struggles with sex. It's just like food – we all know about healthy diets, and eating too much or too little – but we every one of us regularly break those rules in some way or other.

Jesus said he had come to bring us life in our sinfulness – often we are hung up trying to get the sin out of our lifelessness. Jesus has paid the price for our recurring habits. He's done it. I have a hunch he's calling us to put less energy into worrying about sin and more energy into doing some real living.

In *Shawshank Redemption* the character of Red says: 'Get busy living, or get busy dying…'

I'm conscious too that sex can be a powerful, manipulative, demeaning tool. Many of us are damaged one way or another along the way. Is it possible to help each other with all that?

And can we joke about all this? It seems to me that humour is a great way of diffusing some of the intensity. I recently attended a meeting of Christian guys where we not only managed to talk about our struggles with sex – we also had a good laugh about it too. Astonishing!

Questions:
1   Jesus said very little about sex – what can we read into that?
2.   Men and women are different – do you think it's easier for women to share their troubles about sex?
3.   Why do you think sex seems so taboo in Christian circles?
4.   Are there other subjects you'd like to hear discussed more in your group or church?
5.   Did the clip make you think about anything else?

Title: Goldeneye – A Leap Of Faith

Theme: Taking a step of faith

Bible refs: Hebrews 11 v 1

Location of clip: 30 secs to 2 mins 10 secs

Film Description:
Pierce Brosnan's first outing as Bond included this memorable moment. All you really need to know is that he's on a mission to save the free world from the threat of tyranny (well gee, now there's a surprise).

Clip Description:
James Bond runs towards the top of a towering dam in the former USSR. The gate clangs open, he dashes through. He runs to the centre of the massive wall, throws down his rope and places his feet on the edge. For a few seconds he teeters on the brink. James looks down. The deadly drop looms hundreds of metres below. Jagged rocks and bone-crunching concrete stare back at him from the valley floor. He's ready. He doesn't flinch. He straightens his body, prepares himself and dives off the dam. There is silence, total silence, as his body cuts through the air and plummets towards the dead floor below. A rope snakes behind him, attached to his ankles, the metres of wall flash by him, as on and on he falls, his body cutting through the air like a discarded rock. As the ground looms large, the rope takes his weight; his body slows, James pulls a gun and aims at the rock floor. The rope reaches its limit and tenses. As he begins to bounce back up he stretches his arms and fires. His aim is true. A small silver grappling hook slams into the concrete below and steadies him in the air. He's ready to pull himself to safety. He is all set to destroy a Chemical Weapons Facility.

Thoughts:
Ever taken a step of faith? Perhaps you're hovering right now, one foot on the dam, one foot in the air. This is not easy stuff. Stepping out with God always feels like you're about to bunji jump with James Bond. And it never seems to get easier. It always seems to be that same tough decision, requiring the same struggle, the same nerves of steel. I once heard of a guy with a healing ministry who said that every time he had to start praying for someone it felt like stepping off a cliff.

If you need some guiding lights, a few Biblical heroes, look no further than Hebrews chapter 12.

It was by faith Noah built his ark... By faith Abraham obeyed when God called him to leave home...

These were tough tasks to do, and Abraham and Noah loom large as good examples of people who took a risk for God. Ruth isn't listed among these heroes but she could well count alongside them. This is what she said to her mother-in-law:

'Wherever you go, I will go, your people will be my people, your God will be my God.'

An incredible promise. How many of us would give up our homes, our friends, our comfort zones and even (shock horror) our religion – in order to lay down our lives for someone else.

These are not easy decisions. Yet we can take them lightly. We can forget that Abraham and Ruth were subject to the same wavering faith that haunts us. One moment strong, the next weak. One moment bold, the next lost and lonely.

Abraham had not gone far before he hit trouble. A famine comes along and the best plan seems to be a holiday in Egypt. Just one problem, Abraham is suddenly scared that Pharaoh will fancy his wife and kill him to get her. So he starts telling lies and Sarah ends up in Pharaoh's harem, while Abraham ends up with lots of pressies from his royal highness. Surely this isn't walking by faith? Of course not. Abraham was on a bad day – or a bad week – or however long it took before God had to intervene and rescue Abraham and Sarah.

The point is – faith comes and goes – you can steel yourself one day and do an amazing thing. And the next day find yourself struggling with life and doing all the wrong things. But Abraham is up there, along with all the other flawed heroes, looking down and saying, 'Keep going – it's worth it!'

Questions:

1.   I recently came across this quote – *The opposite of faith is not doubt – it's certainty.* Do you agree?
2.   Can you recall times when you stood on the brink and took a leap of faith? Can you tell others about this?
3.   Can you recall times when you missed the chance to step out in faith?
4.   It's not always easy to know whether the challenge to step out in faith is from God or just your own idea. What do you think about this?
5.   Did the clip make you think about anything else?

Title: Much Ado About Nothing - The Hallmarks Of Heaven

Theme: What will heaven be like?

Bible refs: Revelation 21 vv 1-4; Zecheriah 9 vv 16 & 17; Genesis 1 vv 26-31 and 2 vv 4-25

Location of clip: 5 mins 3 secs to 9 mins

Film Description:
This is Kenneth Brannagh's version of William Shakespeare's play.

Clip Description:
This is the opening credit sequence. Benedick and the other men ride back from battle to visit Beatrice and the other women. The sun is shining, the land is fruitful, there is laughter and love in the air. As the men ride onto the estate the women run inside and grab hasty showers. The men dismount and dive into a communal bath. Everyone puts on clean clothes and spruces up to greet one another. It's a place of respect; a place of joy, exuberance, extravagance and splendour.

Thoughts:
What is your idea of heaven? The Bible gives us a variety of glimpses. Isaiah saw winged creatures and flying scrolls. John saw a place without tears and pain and angst. Zecheriah paints a picture of a land where the people will sparkle like jewels in a crown. Everyone will be young and beautiful and men and women will thrive on an abundance of grain and new wine. Not unlike these images of life and laughter, abundance and extravagance in *Much Ado...*

But not all the Biblical images are immediately uplifting. Some can all be a little confusing and at worst – terrifying. This strange mythical place where creatures covered in eyes perform repetitive tasks, and strange coloured horses are ridden by justice and death.
But perhaps some of those descriptions were rooted in contemporary allegory. John in particular sees an astonishing tale of war and slaughter, fire and fear. I wonder if he lay on his back and saw it all played out on the sky, rather like watching *Independence Day*, *War of the Worlds* or *Star Wars*. One thing's for sure, if it were filmed and released in cinemas today it would be 18 rated and not that palatable for many of us.

But the prophecies foretold in Revelation don't tell us too much about the nature of paradise, they show us future events that will bring one world to an end and open the door for a new one. These are images to help people imagine the unimaginable and to spur on those who were and are struggling with pressure and persecution.

What will forever look like?

I guess we all have a hunger in our hearts that reflects something of heaven. A desire for peace and harmony, for creativity and prosperity, for goodness and hope. My fear is that heaven will be like the longest church service in history. Aggggghhh!

It helped me a few years ago when a friend of mine pointed me back to the original picture of paradise. The Garden of Eden, the place where people were originally intended to live with God forever. That was a place of beauty and growth, life and colour, activity and sunshine. This life is now a pale reflection of God's intended vision – but it still bears some resemblance and holds many clues to the future.

It still has the hallmarks of heaven.

Questions:
1.   What would you love to see in heaven?
2.   Do you think we are too preoccupied with the afterlife as Christians?
3.   Have a look at Genesis 2 vv 4 - 25. What clues do we have here regarding everlasting life with God?
4.   Does the thought of heaven inspire or worry you?
5.   Did the clip make you think about anything else?

Title: About Schmidt – Forgiving And Forgetting

Theme: Forgiving one another

Bible refs: Matt 6 v 12; Matt 9 vv 1-6; Matt 18 vv 21-35

Location of clip: 1 hour 8 mins to 1 hour 9 mins 28 secs

Film Description:
Warren R Schmidt has just retired, after decades in the same job at Woodmen of the World Insurance Company. Within a few weeks his wife dies unexpectedly and suddenly Warren is plunged into a completely different way of living. He's a free man. Not only this, but as he clears out his wife's things he discovers old love letters from his best friend. The terrible truth dawns – Warren's wife had an affair with Warren's best friend.

Clip Description:
Warren climbs aboard his new winnibago and takes off on a road trip. On the way he passes a phone booth and decides to call his best friend to forgive him for the affair with his wife. However, instead of a real person Warren encounters an answerphone. He leaves a message, then gets confused and accidentally deletes it. He panics. What should he do now? In the end he does nothing. Technology defeats him. He did his best to forgive his friend, but the forgiveness got erased. Or did it?

Thoughts:
Forgiving people can be hard work. I don't know if you're like me, but I often have to screw up my courage in order to approach someone either to say sorry, or to forgive them. Actually, as I write this I realise I rarely go up to people to forgive them. Somehow I make myself feel it surely must all be my fault. Forgiving them seems to me to be somehow presumptuous or arrogant – somehow unchristian – it means putting the blame on them.

But Jesus spoke much about forgiveness. He told the disciples to forgive others and they would in turn be forgiven.

Forgiving and forgetting are, of course, two different things, and though we may never forget, if we forgive we may well turn the memory into something else, something useful we can pass onto others, instead of something harmful that festers away until the end of time. It's been said that harbouring unforgiveness is like drinking poison yourself and waiting for the other person to die. And the only thing harder than forgiving is the opposite. We often do a lot more damage to ourselves than to the person we are wishing to hurt. Some people build their entire lives around revenge for a particular injury they once received. It becomes a goal for them, a lifestyle chiselled around pain and punishment.

Don't get me wrong – I'm not belittling the pain inflicted upon us by others. It's very real, and very painful. But it's also very damaging. It really can be like collecting an ever-growing pool of poison in our guts. Like acid it seeps into our being and eats away at our happiness and our health. Asking for forgiveness and giving it out requires so much courage. But Jesus knew that. He wasn't asking us to do something he wasn't prepared to do himself. He had to hang on a barbed tree looking like a piece of raw meat, his body oozing blood and death because of what we'd done to him – and somehow, deep down in the core of his being he found the strength to say, 'Please forgive them God, they just have no idea what harm they're doing.'

Questions:
1. Can you recall times when you have plucked up courage and asked for forgiveness from someone you've hurt?
2. We often judge others harshly and forget our own faults. For example, when we are driving it's so easy to judge the others on the road. Have you been guilty of this? Perhaps? Maybe…
3. Are there people that have hurt you?
4. Have you ever considered how hard it may have been for Jesus to say, 'Father, forgive them.'?
5. Did the clip make you think about anything else?

Title: Big Fish – Two Roads

Theme: Choosing the alternate way

Bible refs: Matthew 7 vv 13 & 14; Matthew 13 v 44

Location of clip: 26 mins 28 secs to 29 mins

Film Description:
Edward Bloom is a man who has lived life to the full. His days have been filled with high living and tall tales. As he nears the end of his life he recounts his adventures to his son William.

Clip Description:
Edward and a local giant head off on the journey of a lifetime. They leave their hometown and soon come to a split in the road. One way is well-travelled, it is safe and easy. But the other road beckons to Edward – a road fraught with danger. He urges the giant to take the wider road while he himself takes the narrow one. He soon encounters dark woods, attacking bees, jumping spiders and clawing cobwebs. But Edward journey's on, he has chosen this way and will not give up.

Years before another man took this way, a poet who has never been seen again, so Edward wants to know, what's at the end of this road. What is it that was so appealing that it was worth all this danger?

Thoughts:
Robert Frost wrote: *Two roads diverged in a wood and I, I took the one less travelled by and that has made all the difference.*
Another writer, Henry David Thoreau wrote, *The mass of men lead lives of quiet desperation.*
(Both poems are quoted in the movie *Dead Poets Society*.)
I wonder if there's a link between these two quotes. Do most of us lead desperate, frustrated lives because we find it too difficult to choose the less travelled road?
Edward chooses the less trodden route and discovers a place of mystery, peace, adventure and satisfaction.

Jesus of course, said something similar, '...the gateway to life is small, and the road is narrow, and only a few ever find it.'
Often the danger we encounter on the narrow road is not quite so romantic as that presented to Edward in *Big Fish*. The road to life is peppered with difficult decisions, hard work, nights of wrestling with doubts and fears, and being misunderstood by so many who have not chosen that road.

65

It can also be laden with boring services, opting out of many activities and much energy expended on trying to be nice, and to get it right.

But are those elements all part of the narrow way? Do we put unnecessary difficulties upon ourselves?

Jesus called this the road to life, and this life he described as a life of fullness. What does that mean? He also talked about dying to ourselves that we might live. Taking up our cross and following.

The narrow road is complex, laden with difficult decisions and a certain amount of soul searching.

JC Ryle wrote in his book *Holiness*:

'Dare to make up your own mind what you believe and dare to have distinct views of truth and error. Never, never be afraid to hold decided doctrinal opinions, and let no fear of man, no morbid dread of being thought party-spirited, narrow or controversial, make you rest contented with a bloodless, boneless, tasteless, colourless, lukewarm, undogmatic Christianity.'

And as Edward says in this clip: 'What I recall of Sunday school was – the more difficult something became, the more rewarding it was in the end.'

Questions:
1. Everyone's narrow road is different. Would you agree with this?
2. Do you think we are presented every day with choices to choose the narrow or wide roads?
3. Does the narrow road always have to be difficult and fraught with danger?
4. Are you facing choices at the moment?
5. Did the clip make you think about anything else?

Title: Commando – Getting Tooled Up For Life

Theme: The armour of God

Bible refs: Ephesians 6 vv 10-18; 1 Corinthians 9 vv 24-27

Location of clip: 1 hour 3 mins 50 secs to 1 hour 4 mins 34 secs

Film Description:
John Matrix is a retired Colonel, he used to be head of a special commando strike team. John has moved to a mountaintop home to live out the rest of his days quietly with his daughter. However, before long she is kidnapped in an attempt to coerce John into working for a gang of criminals. Colonel Matrix has just a few short hours to foil the gang's plans and get his daughter back alive.

Clip Description:
John Matrix paddles his dinghy out of the sea, and drags it onto a beach near the bad guys' headquarters. He runs up the sand, dragging the boat until he finds a spot to hide it. He pulls out boxes of weapons and equipment. The boat is loaded with this stuff. He paints camouflage on his face and arms, puts on body armour and belts of bullets and grenades, then snaps his gun together and stands ready to go. He is ready for action.

Thoughts:
When Paul was writing to the Ephesians he was in prison. He wanted to pass on to them a list of the things which are important in life. I guess he looked around for a useful analogy and spotted the armed guards. Maybe he wanted to appeal to the men in that church, maybe he found the analogy helpful himself. Either way, he draws a picture for us, describing salvation, truth, righteousness (or justice), faith, peace, the word of God and the Spirit of God as pieces of armour, weapons in warfare.

On another occasion Paul uses the analogy of athletes, people in training, in competition, pressing on to win their prize and achieve their goal.

I gained a whole new understanding of *the armour of God* when I found this clip. The image Paul uses is a contemporary one for him, it's an exciting one, suggesting action, battles, suspense and victory. It occurred to me that we need modern analogies – ways of seeing again these tools for living. It's not the armour that's important – it's the peace, truth, righteousness etc. Looking at the armour this way gives us a new perspective on it too. The armour becomes something which is not just protection that I wear, but instead it's a set of weapons I can use to fight for good in the wider world.

Any number of analogies might fit. A bag of school books for students, a box of tools for a carpenter or a mechanic. A palate for an artist, a suit for an office worker; a pile of kitchen appliances or a desk set.

What's important is that the analogy connects with us today – presumably Paul hoped that whenever these Christians saw Roman soldiers walking around it would remind them of the important list he gives them. We never see Roman soldiers now – so what picture would be useful for you? What do you see every day that you could use to help you remember that, and any other lists (e.g. the fruit of the Spirit), which matter in life.

Questions:
1. Perhaps it seems daft to draw these modern comparisons. Yet surely the picture of the armour of God was probably a strange one when it was first used?
2. What is the modern equivalent of the armour for you? What will help you remember these important things?
3. Paul says, 'Pray at all times.' What on earth does that mean?
4. What other lists are useful for healthy living?
5. Did the clip make you think about anything else?

Title: Wimbledon – Are You Thinking What I'm Thinking?

Theme: The things we think

Bible refs: Ephesians 4 vv 6-9; Romans 7 vv 22-25

Location of clip: 18 mins 58 secs to 20 mins 46 secs

Film Description:
Peter Colt is a typical British tennis player, talented, struggling and way down the world rankings. He's decided this is to be his last year at Wimbledon; he's going to retire. However, his luck seems to be on the turn. His form holds up and he wins his first match. Suddenly he has a real chance of making his mark.

Clip Description:
Peter is in his second round match, but he has slept too little the night before. His problem is he's in love with one of the female players and he spent the night with her – doing *research*. Now he's in trouble. He's up against the winner of the French Open and all he's won so far is three games. What goes through his mind at a time like this? Well, first up, 'I'm so tired...' 'Then he has an argument with himself about whether he's done a good job progressing this far before losing to his opponent - the French Open Champion.

Thoughts:
I remember a line from a Steve Turner poem entitled *Here Am I:*
'...the thoughts are uncontrollable, some of them hate each other...'
Those words came to me with such power. So many of my thoughts, all through my life have been uncontrollable, hating each other. Thinking good things one second, appalling things the next.

I often look around in church and wonder what is really going on in people's minds. If they're anything like me they have the amazing capacity to think something holy one moment and something horrific the next!

Sex, slander, praise, criticism, compassion, passion, regret, excitement, remembrance, guilt, peace, inspiration, frustration and frivolity all rage against one another in my head. Sometimes in the same moment. Some days my mind can be like trench warfare.
Often I'm not thinking what you think I'm thinking.

The Bible offers us hope – Paul suggests we take every thought captive, and on very bad days I have attempted to do just that.

But it's no mean achievement is it?

God tells us his thoughts are higher than ours. He is not caught up with the petty squabbles that stalk the gloomy corridors of our thinking.

When Paul writes to the Romans he describes the war within his mind. He wants to do what is right, but the old law is still at work in his life. If even Paul battled with his thoughts, I think it's okay that we often struggle.

The irony, of course, is that God sees clearly the mess that is our minds and, to play on words here, he doesn't seem to mind. The cross has taken care of the grimy stuff, and he loves the originality and uniqueness of the other stuff. We often fear to speak out what's really on our minds but sometimes it may deepen our relationship with God, and if we have the courage to tell others, it may deepen our relationship with people too.

Questions:
1. Have you ever considered the possibility that other peoples' thoughts may be as wild as your own?
2. What do you think it really means when Paul talks of 'our minds being renewed'?
3. When it comes to getting it right or wrong - how much do our thoughts matter?
4. What are you thinking right now? Does it amaze you to think that God knows anyway and is completely accepting of you?
5. Did the clip make you think about anything else?

Title: Perfect Storm – Will Your Anchor Hold

Theme: Security and storms

Bible refs: Psalm 55; Luke 8 vv 23 & 24; Isaiah 28

Location of clip: 1 hour 45 mins 44 secs to 1 hour 48 mins 30 secs

Film Description:
Billy Tyne, captain of a sword-fishing boat, is highly competitive and in a bad way because he's not caught much lately. Though the weather is about to turn bad he decides to go out on one more trip. Bad idea. A killer storm is just about to hit the North Atlantic. At first they catch little except a lot of ugly storm warnings, but they persist and the fish start to take the bait. Then – surprise surprise - a storm comes along.

Clip Description:
The boat is at sea and trying to sail home through the mother of all storms. The waves grow, the ocean swells, the boat tosses about like discarded litter in a rainstorm. They hang onto the wheel, bellow, swear, holler at the brooding sky, but the weather rages on, flicking their boat about like a toy. A wall of water rises up to meet them. Their fists clench white, their teeth are bared, their faces set like flint, but it's not enough. This monster will defeat them. This monster will swallow them whole and drag them down to the murky depths of bleak, watery death. There's no way out. Before long the battle is lost. It's all over.

Thoughts:
Storms come in all shapes and sizes, not all of them windy and watery. One thing is for sure – sooner or later we all get hit by one. Like the Psalmist we pray for protection, we pray for deliverance; but like the psalmist we often have to grit our teeth and battle through.

My wife and I went through a storm of one sort the night our daughter was born. Lynn went into labour at 4 o'clock one Tuesday morning and didn't come back from that peculiarly female territory until mid-day on Wednesday. Thirty-two Hours she battled that particular storm, the worst of it in the wee small hours of the night. Storms are always at their bitterest in the dark aren't they?
We had prayed for an easy delivery, pleaded for little pain, put in an appeal for a quick birth. (I'd even been praying for a self-cleaning baby.) Sadly it was not to be. Two epidurals and a lot of hard drugs later our gorgeous daughter popped out. Thirty-two hours of blood, sweat and tears. Literally.

But there was a shining light amidst the darkness. A clue that God was doing what he does best.

We went through three midwives during that one delivery (they kept changing shifts, we weren't killing them off), all of them fantastic, but the one who was there for the bulk of the time, through most of the dark night, was a lovely Christian woman. And even as I write this now, it honestly moves me to tears to think about it. God gave us a friend to see us through. There were no major miracles that night, excepting of course the one colossal miracle of a wriggling, curious, wide-eyed new life born into the world. God often doesn't come through with the Pow! Zap! that we long for, rather the honest reminder that he's there with us, right beside us, caring, struggling, crying, shouting – urging us on.

Urging us to keep battling whenever those storms come our way.

Questions:
1. Jesus calmed the storm in the gospels in dramatic fashion. Have you seen that kind of calming of your own storms? Or has there been help in other ways?
2. What are the anchors in your life - the people or things that keep you going?
3. Do you need more stability?
4. What storms are you facing at present?
5. Did the clip make you think about anything else?

Title: Notting Hill – I Just Want to Be Loved

Theme: God longs for us to love him

Bible refs: Deuteronomy 11 vv 13 & 22; Mark 12 v30

Location of clip: 1 hour 35 mins 10 secs to 1 hour 42 mins 34 secs

Film Description:

Will runs a travel bookshop in Notting Hill. His is a quiet life with not much happening but he has good friends and enough work to keep him out of mischief.

That is until the day Anna Scott walks into his bookshop. Anna is beautiful and Will is in love. One problem; Anna Scott is a film star. She comes from another planet entirely.

Will is smitten and, against all the odds, the two get to know each other and begin to fall in love. However, Anna's dramatic lifestyle whisks her in and out of London faster than a jumbo jet and Will is often left alone, twiddling his thumbs with his head spinning. On one occasion he even bumps into her current Hollywood boyfriend. This can never work. She's playing with him. Will lives in Notting Hill, Anna lives in Beverly Hills. How could he ever have expected it to work?

Clip Description:

Anna comes to see Will. She has bought him a present, a painting that he loves. She bumbles and fumbles her way through the conversation. She wonders if it might be possible to see Will again, perhaps a little, perhaps a lot?

Will is diffident and unmoved. He has seen sense now and knows this cannot work. He may want it to work but they live in two different worlds. He can't stand any more heartache and disappointment. He fears that his poor heart cannot live with anymore failure in the love department.

Anna looks at him and nods.

'Good decision,' she says, 'good decision.'

Then she delivers the knockout punch, or rather a series of stunning jabs to his chest.

She tells him that the fame thing isn't real. It's all nonsense. False.

She says that, at the end of the day, she's just a girl, standing in front of a boy, asking him to love her. And then she leaves, leaving Will confused and bewildered.

Thoughts:

The fame thing isn't real. Over the years we have dressed God in all kinds of clothes, given him all kinds of names and places and personae,

73

disguised him with many kinds of fame.

I remember a line I read years ago; God looks down on his people and says,

'You know, sometimes when I hear them talk about me... I don't recognise myself.'

We concoct all kinds of ways to express our faith. We tell people they must speak in tongues or they mustn't speak in tongues. We tell them they must wear this or wear that, kneel down, stand up, put their hands down, put their hands up. We tell them to describe themselves as born again or spirit-filled or evangelical or charismatic. We instruct them on the many ways to *really* be a Christian, ways to *really* read the Bible, *really* love their neighbours, *really* do church or *really* be evangelistic.

In all this I wonder if we forget one thing.

God just wants to be loved. He longs for relationship. His ideal world involved a man and a woman and time spent with them in a garden.

He's just our God standing in front of us, asking us to love him.

When he spent all that time conversing with Moses.

When he gave us all those messages through the weird prophets of the Old Testament.

When he came to visit Babel to see what was going on with that tower.

When he delivered his people from Egypt and led them to a new free country.

When he sent his son to walk about, eat food, tell stories and turn over tables.

When he sent his spirit to warm our hearts and make us ever hungry for more of him.

When he showed John the sad state of the world, and the promise of a new one to come.

He was just God, standing in front of his people, asking them to love him.

That's the heart of it. Revivals come and go, worship trends swell and die, great preachers and good teachers rise and fall, but the song remains the same.

'Love me with all your heart, with all your mind, with all your soul and with all your strength.'

Surely everything else grows out of that. Doesn't it?

Questions:
1. Augustine said, 'Love God and do what you like.' What do you think he meant by that?
2. We are sometimes in danger of reducing God to a system, a machine

- a jukebox where we attempt to push the right buttons to get the right results. Do you sometimes do this?
3.   What helps us to see again the God who loves us and wants to be loved?
4.   Is it frightening to see God in this way, loveable, vulnerable, approachable?
5.   Did the clip make you think about anything else?

Title: The Matrix – Just How Far Does The Rabbit Hole Go?

Theme: Freedom of choice to follow or not

Bible refs: John 14 vv 25-35; John 3 v 16

Location of clip: 24 mins 8 secs to 28 mins 21 secs

Film Description:
Where do I start? The Matrix is nothing if not complicated.
Mr Anderson lives in the real world. Except he's not Mr Anderson and it's not the real world. The world, this world you and I think is real, is just a computer programme. The real world is hidden from our eyes and looks very different.
Mr Anderson discovers he has another name, he is Neo and he is 'the one'. The one who's destiny is to save the world from the power of the computer programme. The power of the Matrix.

Clip Description:
Neo is visited by the beautiful Trinity. He encounters her in a nightclub and from there she takes him to an old broken-down building, and leads him up a spiral staircase to two huge wooden doors. She opens them and gestures for him to enter. He goes in and meets Morpheus who takes two pills from a box. A red pill and a blue pill. Neo has a choice. He can either take the blue pill, forget everything he's been told and just wake up back in non-reality again; or he can take the red pill and find out 'how deep this rabbit hole goes…'
Neo takes the red pill.

Thoughts:
Freedom of choice is one of the greatest gifts we possess. It's also one of the most frustrating and disturbing. We all have gifts and talents and many of us have the freedom to choose what we do with them. Most people live in splendid obscurity and inflict their anonymous, unique talents on their friends and family and work colleagues.
Some rise to fame and use their talents to do incredible good.
Others sink to appalling levels of infamy and use what they have to perpetrate intolerable acts of evil.
People have often wondered why God does not just destroy those who choose ways of evil.
Well, he did that once, and it didn't work. He sent a flood and wiped the evil people clean off the face of the earth. As Noah came out of the ark to a fresh planet it was as if God wanted to start again from scratch. He renewed his promises and guidelines, those he'd once given to Adam and

Eve. Things would be better this time. Only they weren't. Within a short space of time they were worse. Wiping evil people from the planet does not eradicate the evil itself. God tried several other solutions to this problem of freewill – in the end he chose something so simple, so straightforward, that no amount of evil could mess it up.

Jesus came to this world and divided the planet in two. He opened his hands and, in effect, offered us the red pill or the blue one.
Choose to follow him (take the red pill) and you'll never be the same again.
Choose to ignore him (take the blue pill) and carry on with the reality you've always had.
Get busy living… or get busy dying. That's the choice he offered.

Some people choose the red pill and then give up.
Some people refuse it then change their minds.
Some people secretly take it and follow Jesus.
Some people start to choose then trip up and stop. Then they start again.
Then stop. Then they start again. Stop, start, stop, start…

Which are you?

Questions:
1. Some people can recall a specific moment of choice. For others it's been a gradual process. How would you describe your spiritual journey so far?
2. Are there times when, like Peter at the feeding of the 5000, you'd like to run the other way but have nowhere else to go?
3. Do you know people who are facing the red pill/blue pill decision at the moment?
4. How can you help them? How can you pray for them?
5. Did the clip make you think about anything else?

Title: Lord of the Rings – I Can Resist Anything Except Temptation

Theme: Temptation

Bible refs: Mark 14 v 38; Luke 4 vv 1-14

Location of clip: 24 mins 28 secs to 28 mins 44 secs

Film Description:
Bilbo Baggins lives in the Shire along with all the other Hobbits. For a long time now he has secretly possessed a ring and it's this that has kept him young.

When Gandalf the wizard comes to visit he sees Bilbo magically disappear at a party and, possessing all kinds of wisdom, Gandalf guesses that Bilbo may have this ring.

However the ring is evil, and down through the ages it has caused much death and destruction. As long as Bilbo has it he is not safe. Evil creatures will come for it and kill Bilbo in order to get it.

Clip Description:
Gandalf appears in Bilbo's home as Bilbo is packing to leave the shire. Gandalf asks him about the ring. Bilbo has it and shows it to Gandalf. They discuss it for a short while, then Bilbo begins to leave. Gandalf asks him for the ring. Bilbo says he has left it on the mantelpiece. Then he stops and realises he still has it. Gandalf asks for it again. Bilbo stares at it, the desire to hang onto it is very great. Eventually he turns his hand and lets it fall to the floor. Bilbo leaves, singing as he goes.

Thoughts:
We all battle with temptation – much more than we let on. Often we delude ourselves. We tell ourselves (and others sometimes) that we are not tempted over certain things when often the truth is the opposite. I love the moment in this clip when Bilbo swears he has left the ring behind. He's sure of it, it's on the mantelpiece; but no, in reality he's still hanging onto it. It's still there, tucked away in his pocket for reference later. I'm like that so often.

Some temptations will haunt us for the rest of our lives. We have to face that fact. Greed, lust, flaring tempers and the desire to gossip hover at our doors like a bad smell.

I love that description in Genesis when God says to Cain: 'Sin is crouching at your door, waiting to pounce, it's out to get you and you've got to master it...'

Sin so often lurks in our doorways doesn't it?

My favourite part of this clip is where Gandalf suddenly looms large, and the room grows dark as his voice rises, then he reduces again and says to Bilbo, 'I'm not trying to rob you... I'm trying to help you.' And Bilbo runs to him and embraces him. We fear God's intervention in our lives will somehow rob us - of freewill, of life, of choice, of pleasure. But he has come to help us, and we need these reminders that we can run to him, now back away.

Of course there are many ways to battle it – some people advocate memorising and quoting bits of the Bible. For me distraction is a good antidote. Well it works sometimes. If I find something else to do, something constructive and healthy, I forget the sin that tempts to overpower me.
But that sounds as if I've mastered the problem.
Sin crouches at my doors, windows, computer, bedside, TV and office. The only solution I can find is the one quoted by Paul in Romans chapter 7. In my own words:
'I do lots of things I wish I didn't do, and I don't do the things I should do. Is there a solution? Thanks be to God, Jesus is the solution. God's son has conquered the power of sin to destroy my life.'

Questions:
1. Often when we are tempted God's grace is there to help us, sometimes in surprising ways. Have you experienced this?
2. When we fall our instinct is to fear God and run from him. Yet God wishes we would run to him. What's your experience?
3. Paul writes about grace abounding where sin abounds - what does this mean?
4. Are there struggles with sin you feel ready to bring to God now? Not necessarily for a quick fix, but for on-going help?
5. Did the clip make you think about anything else?

Title: Fever Pitch – What Floats Your Boat?

Theme: Passion

Bible refs: Matthew 22 vv 36-38

Location of clip: 1 hour 27 mins to 1 hour 29mins 36secs

Film Description:
This film is about football and if you know anything about the beautiful game you'll know that the fans can be passionate to the point of madness. The story follows the ups and downs of two love affairs; one - Paul and Sarah, two - Paul and Arsenal. I'm not a football fan but I enjoy this film for two reasons. Firstly the triangular relationship between Paul and football and Sarah and secondly because this is a film loaded with passion, life and heartache.

Clip Description:
It is the last match of the 1989 season between the two teams occupying first and second place in the league. This is the crucial title decider: Arsenal are playing Liverpool. Paul and his best mate are watching the game, but the tension becomes too much. As well as Arsenal being on the verge of losing, some unkind soul keeps ringing the doorbell. Suddenly Paul twigs who it is. Sarah is downstairs waiting on the doorstep. Paul gets up and leaves the room but he's too late; Sarah has gone. And to add insult to injury, while he's away Arsenal score one last time. Against all the odds they have won the league in the dying moments of the match and the final seconds of the season. It's a dream beyond a dream. Paul returns faster than a speeding bullet and the two guys go mental. Outside Sarah walks down the street as jubilant fans pour out of their houses to celebrate.

Thoughts:
What makes you angry? What makes you leap around with ecstasy? What makes you cry? What makes you shout? What makes you care?

Jesus cared so much about the house that was supposed to be dedicated to loving his Father, that when he found it being abused he lost his rag, made a whip and trashed the place. His passion erupted, his anger spilled over like molten lava when he saw the religious leaders making life harder for the poor and oppressed, holding back the access to God, locking the doors to grace.
God wanted to be close to his people. He had appointed a place where they could meet him. How the hell could these cheap money grabbers

dare to turn it into a lucrative and corrupt business? God was freely available to people and yet these scabs were charging the earth for the opportunity.

On other occasions it was the blatant lack of compassion for the poor, or the overlooked . Or the crass behaviour of the hypocrites and the selfish religious leaders. Jesus cared too much to be mild and meek. There was too much at stake. He let his passion spill out, battering the corrupt and enlivening their victims. He laughed wildly at parties. He expressed amazement when people showed great faith. He fumed exasperation when they couldn't see the gift of God right in front of their noses.

There were times when Jesus was not well-behaved. He was never afraid of disrupting the status quo.
If he were around today he would most likely sit down with the homeless and engage in conversation with strangers on the London Underground.
He would be laughing in the pubs and chatting in the parks.
His enthusiasm and passion for life and justice knew no bounds.

Questions:
1. What makes you shout and rant and leap up and down? Are their clues there pointing to what you care about?
2. Do you think it's appropriate to be badly behaved sometimes?
3. What does fullness of life mean to you?
4. What holds us back from letting our passion out?
5. Someone once said, 'Church is often mild-mannered people, telling other mild-mannered people how to be more mild-mannered.' What do you think?
6. Did the clip make you think about anything else?

Title: Saving Private Ryan – The Man Is The Mission

Theme: Why do we do evangelism?

Bible refs: John 4 vv 4 – 26; Luke 19 vv 1-9

Location of clip: 58 mins to 1 hour 1 min

Film Description:
On the 6th June 1944 Private James Ryan and two of his brothers are part of the invasion force sent to liberate France. Ryan's two brothers are killed on the beaches of Omaha and Utah. A week earlier a third brother was killed in New Guinea. James Ryan's mother is about to receive three telegrams informing her that three of her sons are dead. Only James remains. He must be saved at all costs. Eight men are dispatched to find and save Private Ryan.

Clip Description:
Captain John Miller leads this small band of brothers on their assignment to rescue Private Ryan. This is a difficult mission, and to be honest, Miller and his men don't quite understand it. Eight men may well end up dying to save just one. Miller usually comforts himself with the thought that for every one man he loses they've saved the lives of eight or ten or twenty others. This mission is the wrong way round, it doesn't make sense.
They find Private Ryan sooner than expected and explain to him that his brothers are dead. It's difficult to bring bad news but Miller does it professionally, he is straightforward and simple. It's his job, it's what he's been sent to do.
Private Ryan is distraught. He breaks down. He can't believe it. He asks how they died and Miller tells him they were killed in action. Ryan's face changes. How could that be? They're still in school. And slowly the truth dawns. This is the wrong Private Ryan – this is James Frederick, not James Francis. Miller and his men get up and move on quickly, leaving the man confused and bewildered.

Thoughts:
Captain John Miller and his men are on a mission. They are taking huge risks, entering enemy territory, dedicating themselves to the job in hand, risking everything, at times laying down their lives. Yet, at the end of the day – they are just acting under orders.
Their hearts aren't in it. They don't really care about saving Private Ryan. They care about the mission – but not the man.

Evangelism is hard. I used to try and do a lot of it. The more I've done the worse I've become. I've often left people bewildered and confused. I think it's because I cared about the evangelism more than I cared about the people I was trying to evangelise. I felt I ought to do it and I felt I out to be seen to be doing it. That was what good Christians did.

I remember attending a course entitled *Contagious Christianity*. For ten weeks we were taught the way to become better missionaries, natural evangelists. We received instructions and followed the rules. Then, at the end, we were reminded that whilst trying to befriend people in order to 'win them for the gospel', we were, of course, not to do it as if we had an agenda! I went ballistic. We'd just spent ten weeks learning 'the agenda' – of course we were going to have an agenda!

When I look at how Jesus did evangelism he does not appear to just be acting under orders. He doesn't deliver shattering news to people and then walk away. Sometimes they walk away from him but he doesn't choose to leave them. He cares about the people more than the mission. When Lazarus dies he doesn't cut to the chase and start straight on with the resurrecting business – he lets his heart shatter first. He crumbles to his knees and sobs uncontrollably because his friend has suffered and died.

When ten lepers come to him for healing he is depressed that only one of them comes back to get to know him better, the other nine are only interested in their healing. Jesus is interested in people. When thousands left him because he wouldn't perform more magic and bake a bit more bread out of thin air, he turned to his disciples and said with sadness, 'Will you leave me too?'
Jesus loves people. His mission is the people: caring for them, getting to know them, listening to them. Without any hidden agenda.

When Jesus gathers his first friends notice that he does not try and convert them or feed them the gospel. All he says is, 'Come with me, and I'll teach you a new trade...' He gathers a group of friends around him and only later worries about informing them about God.

Questions:
1. How do you find doing evangelism - difficult or easy?
2. I worked in a cinema for 18 months and never told anyone I was a Christian. Do you relate to that at all?
3. Are there people who may be close to the kingdom who you care deeply about?
4. Have you considered the many different ways you can evangelise - gentle, subtle, practical ways?
5. Did the clip make you think about anything else?

Title: Cinema Paradiso - No Sex Please, We're Christians

Theme: What should we read, watch and look at

Bible refs: Philippians 4 v 8; 1 Corinthians 7 v 31

Location of clip: 8 mins 9 secs to 10 mins 39 secs

Film Description:
Salvatore loves films. He spends every spare minute in the local cinema with Alfredo, the projectionist. He watches all the movies that come through there and Alfredo instills in him a lifelong love of film. The local priest also watches the movies. In fact, the priest watches them long before anyone else does.

Clip Description:
The priest is sitting in the cinema while Alfredo runs a copy of the latest new movie. He enjoys the film, but every time a scene involving kissing comes along he rings a bell furiously. The projectionist rips off a sliver of paper and jams it in the reel at that point so that later he can go through the film and cut out the naughty moments.
The people of the town must not be subjected to this wanton snogging. It is not good for them. The priest must first view the film and edit out every single scene of this nature.

Thoughts:
What should we watch? This is a thorny issue and it becomes thornier as the days go by. Many popular movies now contain swearing, violence and sex scenes. Read the small print on any 12A rated movie and you will probably find that it contains one use of *strong* language. That's often how the makers get the film bumped up into the more adult-appealing 12 rating, by including one use of the *F* word. (It always annoys me that they call it strong language – perhaps *weak* would be a better description? What do you think? Discuss... unless you're alone in which case it's probably best not to – you might just be considered mad!)

I have compiled a jumbled collection of thoughts on this issue, and here they are:

• Paul said: 'Whatever is true, noble, righteous etc... think on these things.' Well, if we are to take that at face value we would not watch anything. The news is selective and biased and often graphic in detail; sport contains scenes of bad behaviour and is often sponsored by dubious companies; the Bible itself is choked with tales of sex and violence - in

84

Ezekiel chapter 16 Israel is described as a naked prostitute lying in a field and covered in blood. And of course our thresholds are different. Don't ask me to watch *Casualty* – it's stuff like that which keeps me awake at night, I don't want to watch happy, healthy people end up sick and sad thanks very much. But I know there are plenty of people who are not harmed at all by watching this.

• The context in which Paul is writing here is one of stress and worry and the peace that fills our minds and lives. If we want to preserve that kind of wellbeing then Paul is encouraging us to know what kind of things disturb us and what good things revive us. And I would suggest this does vary from person to person.

• Paul himself was clearly in contact with things of the world. In 1 Corinthians he advises, 'those in frequent contact with the things of the world should make good use of them, without becoming attached to them.' In the Old Testament, in Chronicles chapter 12 verse 32, there are a bunch of discerning guys known as The Men of Issachar who, to quote the good book, 'understood the temper of the times and knew the best course for Israel to take.' I would suggest that there are people like that today, women and men called to understand and engage with 'the temper of the times'.

• Jesus was in contact with the things of this world, steeped in them in fact, and he advised that it's not what you put into a person that affects them, it's what comes out. (Check out Matthew 15 v 11)

• Biblical Christianity is not about building safe-houses where we can run and hide from the reality around us, but rather about making inroads into the various and diverse places in our world.

• When Paul went to Athens he looked at the art around him and skilfully used the statues and poetry he encountered to point people to the living God. He did this quite brilliantly with their statue to the unknown God, offering to help them understand the God they are already worshipping.

• In Ezekiel chapter four God is prepared to go much further than Ezekiel to communicate with his people. He asks the prophet to cook food over human excrement, but Ezekiel is horrified and pleads not to have to do this as it would defile him, so God relents and says he may use cow dung.

Movies are asking real questions about life, questions we often shy away from in church circles. Movies are the parables of our day; the popular media available for us to draw upon for examples and analogy.

(But you know that – you've bought this book!)

Now I do understand that we must still be careful, and many things in movies can be harmful and unhelpful but that's where we must seek, knock, search and use our intelligence.

Questions:
1. Have you thought through your own boundaries? Are you aware of what disturbs you and what does not?
2. Jesus told violent stories - e.g. the Good Samaritan and The Tenants in the Vineyard. Ezekiel described Israel in terms that were shocking and violent. Hosea and Song of Songs contain strong themes of a sexual nature. If we filmed these passages they would be 18 rated. What do you think about this?
3. Some films may not be nice - but niceness is not the same as holiness. What do you think?
4. Do you find that your discomfort when watching some films varies depending on the people you are watching it with?
5. Did the clip make you think about anything else?

Title: Deep Blue Sea/Jaws – Just When You Thought It Was Safe To Be A Prophet

Themes: Jonah; evangelism

Bible refs: Jonah chapters 1-4

Location of clip: *Deep Blue Sea* - 28 secs to 3 mins 42 secs; *Jaws* – The opening sequence

Film Descriptions:

Deep Blue Sea – a team of researchers breeds the most dangerous fish in the world. By re-jigging the genetics of one or two mako sharks they inadvertently create a devastating aquatic killing machine. A storm hits, the floating laboratory begins to fall apart and before you can say *'this was no boating accident'* the place is awash with murderous free-swimming radicals. The scientists spend the rest of the movie attempting to stay alive.

Jaws - a great white shark has decided to holiday in Amity bay. This creates panic on the beach and a massive headache for police chief Brody. The first he knows about it is when the head and shoulders of a young woman are washed up on the beach. Before you can say *'you're gonna need a bigger boat'* would-be shark catchers take to the high seas in dinghies and fishing boats and you can bet it's all going to end in tears. I still can't go swimming without thinking of this film and what sharp fangs might just be lurking beneath those cold waves.

Clip descriptions:

DBS – Four young lovers enjoy a bottle and a smooch on their woefully inadequate raft. Before you know it things start going bump in the water and they're under attack from an enemy below. Drinks, teddies and ghetto blasters all get washed overboard, closely followed by real people. They splash about in the water for a while and you know that sooner or later limbs will be lacerated. Or will they?

Jaws - Two friends go swimming in the sea way past dark. They both remove their clothes and the girl runs in while the man collapses on the beach. The girl swims in the water for a while, oblivious of the danger lurking beneath. She stops to tread water for a while. Suddenly she feels a tug on her body. She reaches down but her hand finds a space where her leg used to be. Suddenly her body thrusts upwards and then disappears into the water.

She has been swallowed by something very nasty indeed.

Thoughts:
'Now the LORD had arranged for a great fish to swallow Jonah. And Jonah was inside the fish for three days and three nights.'
Never have two short sentences created so much debate for so long for so many people.
Did Jonah really get swallowed by a big fish? Was it a whale? Was it a shark?
Or is the whole thing just a parable?
One thing's for sure, parable or not, it's loaded with vital lessons.

This story is most often used as a guide for evangelism: think of a city, any city, and go and try and convert it. But usually that doesn't make us better missionaries – it just makes us feel guilty.
In spite of our extravagant desires to 'take this city for Christ' evangelism is often a one-to-one thing (crowd conversion doesn't really work) Jesus's model seems to be find one person who's interested and give them your full attention.

It's worth noting that a) Jonah was a prophet and b) he had a clear directive from God. Converting cities wasn't something everyone was supposed to do. Israel was called to light up the world by living differently as a nation, demonstrating a healthy, caring, alternative lifestyle which would show other nations the nature of their caring, healthy God. Bear in mind that every nation had their gods, so it was a given that your god or gods would influence your living.

But I digress... Let's consider Jonah's good points; he was courageous, he's the one who insists the sailors throw him overboard and they have to be practically pummelled into doing it. This display of courage must surely have encouraged their conversion. And talking of conversions he was pretty good at it, wasn't he? I'm not sure if there are any other Biblical heroes who managed to turn an entire malevolent population back to God. And of course, like Moses, Jonah is brutally honest. If it was me I'd probably say the right things, 'Yes God, I'd love to go and convert the vile and dangerous Ninevah. It'll make my day.'
Then I'd dive under the bed with my mobile phone and quietly order a one way ticket to Tarshish.
But not Jonah. Not only does he openly run away, but when he repents and goes to Ninevah he then openly vents his anger and frustration that things didn't go the way he hoped.
Presumably he thought that it would be of some consolation to watch Ninevah burn. So when it doesn't it's blooming annoying. It's not fair.

Ninevah's horrible. They should all die! And Jonah tells God this – no messing.
And then the final straw. Jonah finds some shelter beneath a plant, but horror of horrors – the whole world's against him! The bloomin' plant collapses and dies. It's not fair!

But there's a message for Jonah here. He *claims* he cares about the plant – but of course it's his own comfort he's really caring about. If he really cared about a plant, surely he'd also care about 120,000 lost souls too. People are people, Jonah, whatever the colour of their eyes or the tone of their skin.

We do tend to get carried away about the wrong things, don't we? There's a legendary tale about a preacher who ingeniously highlighted this. So here's my version. A preacher once described the way 400 children die every month in a single slum in Kenya.
'400!' he said, 'And yet most of us don't give a shit about this. In fact we care more about the mention of the word shit than we do about the 400 children.'

What really matters in life? Jonah had to learn a tough lesson about all that.
But let's not forget that he was courageous, honest and passionate, and wherever he went people were converted. Almost in spite of Jonah.

Questions:
1.   What makes you angry in life?
2.   Can you identify at all with Jonah's running away?
3.   Jonah was a gifted prophet - speaking about his faith was his gift. Your gift may not be speaking at all - what gifts do you have that God can use?
4.   What encourages you to share your faith? What enables you to do it better?
5.   Did the clip make you think about anything else?

Title: French Kiss – That's Outrageous!

Theme: The prodigal son

Bible refs: Luke 15, John 3 v 16

Location of clip: 1 hour 23 secs to 1 hour 3 mins 3 secs

Film Description:
Kate's life is in chaos. Her fiancée has dumped her for a French girl he met on a business trip. Determined to get him back she jumps on a plane and flies after him. On the trip over she meets Luc, a beguiling French thief and con man. The two strike up an unlikely and reluctant partnership. On their journey together they discover there's a lot more to each other than they ever imagined.

Clip Description:
Luc is on his way home, back to the family vineyards. He and Kate stop at a café for a drink. A strange car pulls up and Luc immediately engages in a fight with the stranger who leaps out. After Luc has floored him he explains to Kate that this is his brother.
Cut to the vineyards. Half of all this majestic land is Luc's - well it would be if he hadn't gambled it all away in single hand of cards.
Luc's family all hate him, he tells Kate, he is too frivolous, too foolish, too impetuous – and he has slept with his brother's wife. They do not want to see him again. They don't want him back.
Just as he is telling her this there is a shout. They turn to see Luc's father standing there, his arms open wide and a welcoming smile on his face.

Thoughts:
God's love is naïve. It's wanton, unnecessary, unfair and indiscriminate. There's nothing like it for annoying people.
We are so used to the idea that acceptance is based on certain conditions. Do this and you'll be okay, do that and you'll be forgiven.
Don't abide by these rules and you'll be shut out.

So when Jesus comes along telling silly stories about wasters who deliberately hurt people and squander the many good things they have – well it's enough to make an older brother go ballistic.
Surely God must be like us? Surely he must be at least mildly annoyed at such sinful behaviour.
You can't go sleeping with your brother's wife and then return home to a warm welcome.
It's just not fair!

But that's the point. God's love is not based on fairness. God's generosity is not based on merit. This is the problem Jesus faced when trying to explain the principals of the Kingdom of God. It's not based on our principals.

The Prodigal is just like Luc. He is not organised or careful, he is selfish and greedy, he is not kind, not caring, not principled. He just lives for himself. He doesn't qualify for any kind of outside help and he knows it. Yet his father is standing there - even as he's mumbling about how much his family hate him - his father is there, arms open, face smiling, voice bellowing 'Welcome home.'

There is an astonishing clip in the movie *To End All Wars* which well sums up this unrelenting love.
Major Ian Campbell and Dusty Miller are enemies. They are both prisoners of the Japanese in the same camp during World War 2. Dusty Miller believes in compassion and peace, Ian Campbell wants to fight back. When Campbell is caught trying to escape he is sentenced to death along with his fellow escapees. They are forced to kneel and the soldiers in the camp prepare to behead them while the rest of the prisoners watch. Each escapee is beheaded then Dusty Miller risks his life and steps forward. He whispers in the Japanese officer's ear. He offers himself in place of Major Ian Campbell. He will die in place of his enemy. The Japanese Commandant knows Dusty Miller is a Christian, so he crucifies him. Miller dies in place of Campbell. He dies for his enemy. It's an incredible parable about the death of Jesus.

The compassion of Jesus has inspired many others to lay down their lives.

Questions:
1. Do you know any prodigals?
2. In Jesus's story the prodigal's brother was fed up about the grace being shown to this scruffy, rebellious kid. Have you ever felt like that? (I often have.)
3. Do you think we make too many demands on people? Do we make it too difficult for the prodigals to return?
4. Are we prepared to welcome the prodigals knowing they may well run away again tomorrow?
5. Did the clip make you think about anything else?

Title: Titanic – Those Known To Be Saved

Theme: Salvation; God's unstoppable rescue operation

Bible refs: Romans 5 vv 6-11

Location of clip: 2 hours 41 mins 20 secs to 2 hours 47 mins

Film Description:
The unthinkable happens. The unsinkable sinks. If you haven't seen this movie – I'd be surprised. It's still one of the most watched yarns on the planet. A collection of folks board a huge, spanking new boat for the ride of a lifetime, what they don't realise is this - for most of them it will be the last ride of a lifetime.

The *Titanic* hits an iceberg and there aren't enough lifeboats. This really was the unthinkable. The *Titanic* was never supposed to sink, it wasn't designed for that, it was just never going to happen.

Clip Description:
The lifeboats are full and rowing away from the bodies that are still floundering in the water. They dare not go back for more as they fear being swamped and the boats sinking. But one brave crew member refuses to row away from the scene of the wreck, instead he stays behind, hollering for any who are left alive. When he hears voices he rows back towards the ship, back into danger, to search for the last survivors.

Thoughts:
I have always found this to be the most moving part of this film. Somebody cares enough to turn back and search for the dying.
It's said that when the *Titanic* went down, a board was placed outside the company office. Each day it carried two lists. *Those known to be lost* and *Those known to be saved*.

When we were utterly helpless – thrashing about in an ice cold sea, waiting to sink forever – Jesus manned that lifeboat and came looking for us. God mounted a mission and sent the one man who could do something to save us from a chilling end. We weren't designed to flounder in sin. Our lives were originally built to prosper, to flourish, to be places of destiny and eternity.

It was only pride that sent us on a collision course with death.

And now we are faced with that most difficult of all dilemmas – the pressure to choose. Making choices is fine – until I have no choice. Then I want to nail my colours firmly to the fence. Stand with a foot in both camps, half of me in the sea, half in the lifeboat. It's almost offensive that people force me to make a decision!

Yet that would have been madness to the folks on the *Titanic* – many of them screamed for hours for the moment when they could choose life. The freedom to choose was the one thing they were desperate for.

One thing is sure – we understand very little about salvation. This in spite of the fact that Jesus told us many stories about it. People were cast out into utter darkness for simple things like not using their talents or not helping the poor.

But one image leaps out at me now. There will be a divine party one day, and it's gonna be the mother and father of all celebrations. Jesus told a story about the invitations going out – and most people refusing them. Then, when the party started, one poor chap decided to try and gatecrash. No dice. He was thrown out like a crumpled coke can. He'd had plenty of opportunity, a lot of warning. Now others had come instead.

I'm often very scared that I'll miss that party but that fear reminds me that I really don't want to miss it. I long to be there with all my being and that longing keeps me looking to the one who's given me a ticket. The one who came back in that boat to rescue this ice-cold, miserable, bedraggled survivor. I didn't earn it, I can't pay for it and I can think of a million reasons why I should be turned away. But by some mysterious gift of grace I have a ticket; I've been rescued.

So what about the unknowns? Those not known to be in either list yet. Those still out there in the grey ocean of uncertainty. Not everyone is yet known to be saved or known to be lost. Jesus spoke of those who were *close to the kingdom*. He saw the most unlikely folks as being on the doorstep, ringing heaven's bell. G K Chesterton once said that a man knocking on the door of a brothel is very close to the kingdom of God.

Questions:
1. When you have doubts about your salvation - what encourages you?
2. Do you know people who are close to the kingdom?
3. Can you remember what it was like to be outside of the kingdom looking in? What drew you closer?
4. Are there practical things you can do to help rescue the folks still floundering in the water?
5. Did the clip make you think about anything else?

Title: Raiders Of The Lost Ark – The Adventure Of Faith?

Theme: Warning: Being a Christian can be boring

Bible refs: Luke 10 vv 17-20

Location of clip: 3 mins 26 secs to 10 mins 36 secs

Film Description:

This is the opening sequence to the greatest action movie ever made (in my humble opinion). Indiana Jones teaches archaeology – and in his spare time he trots the globe chasing priceless artefacts and fighting bad guys. *Time Team* this is not!

Clip Description:

Indy enters a cave in search of long lost treasure. He is accompanied by a very frightened South American guide. But Indy does not see the danger, he simply has his eyes on the prize. Somewhere beyond these labyrinthine corridors, and deadly traps there is a cavern, and that's where he will find what he's looking for. Indy presses on, being assaulted along the way by poisonous spiders, razor sharp spears, false floors and hidden snares.

Suddenly here is it is – the cavern, and there on a large stone plinth lies the treasure. Indy pulls a bag of sand from his pocket, judges it to be a little heavier than the artefact and so pours some sand away, then slowly, oh so slowly, he reaches for the prize. In a second he scoops it up and replaces it with the bag of sand. All is well. Nothing happens. They are safe, and Indy has the treasure. Ah! But I spoke too soon. The cave begins to rumble and the ground begins to shake. Indy wasn't quick enough, the plinth was spiked, removing the treasure has triggered a minor earthquake, the walls begin to tremble and the roof starts to crumble. Poison darts fly from holes in the walls and the cave floor gives way. Indy and the guide turn and flee, Indy shoving the treasure into his bag as they go. Rocks fly as they leap and dive through the shuddering cave. At one point the guide tricks him into parting with the prize, then leaves Indy stranded. But Indy leaps over a massive gap in the cave floor, dives under a descending wall and regains the artefact from the guide who has been spiked by hidden spears. Then, chased by a giant boulder, Indy speeds out of the cave and into the safety of the daylight.

Except it's not safe. He finds himself surrounded by locals armed with bows and arrows, and his arch enemy Belok takes the precious treasure from him. Indy turns tale and flees, the local Indians close on his tail.

Thoughts:

I have often made the mistake of describing Christianity as a bit of an adventure. To hear me talk sometimes you'd think it was like a never-ending summer blockbuster, full of thrills and spills, with every Christian as the indomitable Indiana Jones, or his hapless sister Bridget.

But that's not true is it? I'd like it to be true, I'd like Christianity to be about action and adventure, and I'd like those outside the faith to be attracted to that. But these days I realise something – I described it in such a way to try and make it sound more attractive to those outside the faith.

Of course, it depends what you mean by adventure. Certainly your life takes a different turn, and all kinds of new possibilities open up before you. But God is rooted in real life, he made normal life, he is at home there. Chances are your '*Christian life*' consists of much of what your '*non-Christian life*' contained. Cooking, cleaning, ironing, 9 to 5-ing, computing and arguing with those closest to you.

There are most likely patches of frustration, moments of elation, nights of despair and days of worry.

If your life is anything like mine it's speckled with laughter, fears, excitement, disappointment and foolishness.

We live with all of these roommates.

Jesus said, 'In this world you will have trouble…'

And he should have known, he had lots of it.

We can be fooled into thinking that the *Christian* life is somehow in another league to normality. That real life is something to be escaped. That we have to struggle to overcome the mundanity of every day life in order to catch glimpses of the vastly superior '*spiritual life*'. But think on this: God made Adam and Eve and put them in a garden. That was his idea of perfect life. Not a place where he had to keep intervening with miracles and thunderbolts but a place where people worked, rested, slept, laughed, loved and had families.

In a way the notion of family provides a good analogy. You could describe having children as being an adventure – there are certainly moments of high drama and days of thrills and spills. But there are also hours of boredom, and days of arguing, weeks of tidying and cleaning, months of worry and years of personality clashes. That does make for an adventure of one sort – but it's not quite the romantic swashbuckling of *Zorro* or the derring-do of *James Bond*.

When the disciples returned from days of casting out demons and healing people Jesus was excited for them and applauded their tales of adventure – but he finished that scene on a realistic note.

'Don't rejoice because the demons obey you – rejoice because your names are written in heaven.'
Nothing can take that away, nothing can change that. Excitement comes and goes, miracles pass and fade – but your name will always be written in heaven.

Questions:
1. Have you ever stopped to consider that God may be speaking to you all the time, through the everyday things - through the people you see in the street?
2. We need inspiring biographies about extraordinary Christians, but does this give us a false impression of life?
3. It has been said that: 'Coincidence is God's way of remaining anonymous.' Have you seen God working anonymously lately? Perhaps we need the perspective of others to enable us to see that sometimes?
4. Can you think of one natural and one supernatural way you have experienced God lately?
5. Did the clip make you think about anything else?

Title: Motorcycle Diaries – Keep Going!

Theme: Perseverance And encouragement

Bible refs: Hebrews 12 vv 1-2

Location of clip: 1 hour 39 mins 5 secs to 1 hour 43 mins 30 secs

Warning: This clip contains swearing

Film Description:
This is the story of Ernesto (Che) Guevara in his student days – when he took a trip with a friend around South America on a Norton motorbike. Che and his mate initially head off in search of action and girls, the preoccupation of a lot of young men. But along the way they meet the poor, the downtrodden, the side-lined – and all of this begins to affect Che.

Clip Description:
Towards the end of their trip they arrive at a colony of leprosy sufferers. There they befriend the leprosy sufferers and the medical staff caring for them. However they get into a lot of trouble as they refuse to wear gloves and have far too much contact with these sick, infectious people.
It is now Che's birthday and he has had a great party with the medical staff, but now he wants to cross the river that divides the colony and go and celebrate with his new friends. However, the river is wide and wild and contains all manner of creatures great and small. Swimming at night is not a good idea, a boat in the daylight would be much safer.
But Che is adamant, this trip has not been about safety, it's been about life. He's going to see his new friends, and he dives in.

The doctors at the colony pile out to see what's going on. They call him back, advise him of the foolish nature of his actions, try and persuade him to give up. But he swims on. As he gets half way one of the lepers on the other side spots him coming and calls to some of the others. The lepers gather together on the other side and shout encouragement.
Keep going, Ernesto! Keep going!' They call to him.
And so Che is caught between two crowds, the doctors and his friend calling him back - and the folks with leprosy calling him on.
On he goes, growing more tired with every stroke but pushing on, still swimming, not giving up, and with every stroke he gets nearer to his friends, nearer to those shouts of encouragement.
Eventually, spluttering and weak, gasping for every breath, he arrives on the far bank and the lepers help him up and out of the water. He has made it.

On the previous side of the river his best friend says, 'I always knew he could do it...'

Thoughts:
The writer of the book of Hebrews describes a group of Old Testament heroes, watching us and urging us on in our faith. He calls them a great crowd, or cloud, of witnesses.

If you look back over Hebrews 11 you will discover they are a strange group – misfits, crooks, liars, cheats, a prostitute – you can read their stories in the Old Testament. Some of them had lots of faith and were killed for it. Others had lots of faith and were rescued because of it.

All of them want you to keep going. It's as if they're saying, 'We made it – it's very hard – but we made it. Keep going, you can do it too. If we can do it – you can'.

I wonder which crowd of witnesses you might have been in on that night Che swam the river. Would you be calling him back, warning him of danger, thinking about the things that make it a bad idea?

Or would you be urging him on, encouraging him to keep going, telling him it's worth the energy and the weariness?

We all need encouragement to keep going. There are times when every day feels like swimming that river. Days when every hour, every minute, feels like battling the torrent.

Keep going. There isn't a single hero in the Bible who did not have to battle with discouragement and trouble. Life is difficult but remember those witnesses – admittedly it's frustrating that we can't hear them! But perhaps occasionally one or two cheers slip through, maybe one or two words echo in our heads. And perhaps, most importantly, they urge us on through someone nearby who offers us a smile, a nod, or a kind word.

Questions:
1. Have you ever considered how important your smile and words of encouragement may be to someone near you? They may feel inconsequential to you – but they may help someone through a difficult day.
2. In the clip, which side of the river would you have been on?
3. Can you name some of the Old Testament heroes who had to wait and persevere?
4. Can you recall lessons you have learnt, or are still learning, from waiting?
5. Did the clip make you think about anything else?

Title: Troy – Heroes And Villains

Theme: Everyone's the same really

Bible refs: Hebrews 11 vv 3-12; Psalm 103 v 14

Location of clip: 13 mins 56 secs to 17 mins 12 secs

Film Description:
Paris and his brother Hector have just visited the Greeks and are now returning home bearing gifts and tales of daring adventure. However, they bear one gift too many. Paris has fallen in love with Helen and is secretly bringing her back to Troy. Now, on the voyage back, he must break the news to his brother. Paris's decision to take Helen will result in all out war against Greece and ultimately the wholesale destruction of Troy.

Clip Description:
Paris meets Helen on a friendly visit to Sparta and they quickly begin an affair. Helen is unhappily married to Menelaus and readily falls for Paris's affections. When Paris and his brother Hector leave for Troy Paris secretly hides her aboard their ship, and now that they are safely at sea he tries to break the news gently to his brother. He begins by discussing the weather, then he asks if his brother still loves him. Hector sees through this and wonders what Paris has done now. Paris takes him below deck and shows him the bad news. Helen is on board. Back in Sparta, Menelaus is furious. His wife is missing and his men inform him that she has sailed with the Trojan princes. Menelaus vows to kill them all.
On board their ship Hector goes wild. He berates Paris for his foolish actions. Paris talks about fighting and love but he really has no idea what he is talking about. He has seduced too many women and never fought in a single battle. He thinks he's a hero, he thinks he is doing a glorious thing. But in reality his actions are selfish and his love is impure.

Thoughts:
Paris is young, foolhardy and impetuous. He is brave but also selfish. He is high-minded but misguided. Principled but cowardly. He talks of love but is about to bring war and death on the entire population of Troy. He is supposed to be serving these people, not destroying them. He talks of dying for Helen but it's others who will do the dying.

King David brought the same trouble on himself. At a time when other kings were fighting to defend their people, he (for whatever reason) finds himself at home, twiddling his thumbs. Perhaps he had a bit of a head cold. Perhaps he was on sabbatical. Whatever - that's when he noticed

99

Bathsheba. Had he seen her on previous nights? Did he watch her take a bath many times, the passion growing within him till he could stand it now more and just had to invite her round for a night-cap? Was he trying to find his identity; prove his manhood by seducing a new woman? Was he seeing if he still had 'it'?

Whatever the truth, one thing is sure, this man who could kill giants, this man who's passionate heart burned like God's own heart, this creative genius – was about to let his dark side take control.

All the Biblical heroes had feet of clay. And not just feet. Hands, eyes, brains, loins… you name it they blundered with it.

Abraham started out well then turned coward and liar when he got to Egypt.

Jacob was a cheat and a liar.

Moses was a murderer.

Joseph was spoiled, self-obsessed and over-confident.

Paul was a killer and a control freak.

By comparison the much-maligned Rahab wasn't so bad. At least her prostitution was out there in the open for all to see.

Why drag up all these bad points? Coz I'm a liar and a cheat, spoilt and self-obsessed, a coward and a potential killer. It heartens me no end to read the many ways God used these mixed up, vital people. To see faith at work in their lives in the midst of their crimes and misdemeanours is good news, isn't it? They were as messy and muddled as me. Their lives had been ambushed by trouble in the same way mine has.

God has always worked with misfits and criminals. He's well used to the challenge.

Even you and I are in with a shout.

Questions:
1. The Bible tells us that God knows we're dust. Psalm 103 v 14 proclaims; 'He understands how weak we are, he knows we are only dust.' Do we expect too much of ourselves?
2. In the clip Paris has high ideals that he can never live up to. Are you like this?
3. Jesus said, 'Be perfect as your heavenly father is perfect.' A friend tells me she thinks he said this with a wry smile on his face, knowing this is beyond us. Indeed, if we were perfect we would no longer need Jesus's costly sacrifice. What do you think about this?
4. Christians are often expected to be good and nice. How do you cope with this expectation?
5. Did the clip make you think about anything else?

Title: Meet The Parents – The Difference Between In-laws & Outlaws

Theme: Family

Bible refs: Ephesians 6 vv 1-4; Genesis 42-44

Location of clip: 23 mins to 27 mins 31 secs

Film Description:
Greg is in love with Pam and visits her family for the weekend in order to propose to her. There's just one catch. He must first ask for her father's permission to marry her, and her father (Jack) is an uptight, ex-CIA, disciplinarian. Greg is desperate for things to go well – but of course, they don't. He and Jack are very different and everything he attempts seems to go badly wrong.

Clip Description:
It's the evening meal and Greg is asked to say grace. He is awkward and has no idea what to say but wants to impress everyone. So in the end he makes up a prayer which lasts longer than the book of psalms and incorporates a song from Godspell. Then he makes a joke about a vase on the mantelpiece only to discover it is in fact an urn containing the ashes of Jack's dead mother. Jack then reads a poem about his mother and Greg is completely lost for words.

Thoughts:
The difference between in-laws and outlaws? Outlaws are wanted. Families and extended families are not always the easiest of places. It's funny that we often describe the church as the family of God, yet rarely take into consideration the fact that a family can be a place of jealousy, grudges, embarrassment, misunderstanding, personality clashes and feuding. Mind you, perhaps that does bare some resemblance to church life, after all!

When Joseph finally got to meet his family at the end of Genesis it seems as if things don't go quite according to plan. It's a dramatic reunion, he loves his brothers but he has a huge agenda too. They did sell him into slavery after all. You know how it often is, you mean to say one thing – but when the moment arises something else pops out. You mean to say sorry but instead perpetuate the problem. You mean to say I love you but the words stick in your throat.

Joe's way out is to plan a practical joke but the whole thing becomes painful and protracted. In the end he threatens to imprison his younger brother Ben to see if his older brothers care more about him than they had

101

cared about Joe - to see if they have reformed their brother-dumping ways.

Families have so much history, and the history can be painful. In his letter to the Ephesians Paul gives advice to children and parents about respect and discipline. Advice that's not easy to re-enact within your family setting. Take Christmas for example. It is held up as a time to be with your wider family but there can be so much planning, spending, and difference of opinion that it ends up being a test of your endurance. Family gatherings can be a time of stress and bewilderment.

I don't know what your family is like. Or your in-laws. It's not so much a question of how much you love them – more a case of how do you cope with all being together? How do you cope with the agenda's left by the past? How do you keep moving on together when you may be the only one who wants to keep moving on at all?

Questions:
1. The church is sometimes referred to as a family. Do you think that's because we idealise family, or because church is a place fraught with the same kind of difficulties?
2. 'We always hurt the ones we love.' Has this sometimes been your experience within your family?
3. It's often said that we clash with those who are most like us. What do you think?
4. How do you work through difficulties with your family? Is it appropriate to pray about them?
5. Did the clip make you think about anything else?

Title: 50 First Dates – Get Off Day One

Theme: Deepening our relationship with God

Bible refs: Hebrews 6 vv 1 & 2

Location of clip: 1 hour 1 min 4 secs to 1 hour 3 mins 19 secs

Film Description:

Lucy has short-term memory loss. Every day her father and her brother reconstruct the same day – her father's birthday – over and over again. Same newspaper, same food, same film, same everything. Every day she lives that same day again and again.

Then Henry comes into her life, and promptly falls in love with her. One problem, she never remembers the following day. So he has to make her fall in love with him again – every single day.

Clip Description:

Gratuitous kissing! Every time Lucy kisses Henry it's her first time. Every kiss is a first kiss for her. Every kiss has the excitement and the mystery of the first time. He may have kissed her thirty times – it will always be number one for her. And as Lucy says: 'There's nothing like a first kiss.'

Thoughts:

In the book of Revelation the message to the church of Ephesus includes the line, 'You've lost your first love.'

It seems to me that this may be misleading for many of us. We so often want to live in the glow of that first exhilaration when we first got to know God, that first experience of his love and his power. Those early days of knowing him. We expend an awful lot of energy trying to feel again what we once felt, trying to sing those songs, get back that emotion. But we never can. And here's the news – we're not supposed to. God wants us to move off day one. If we stay there we are stuck. We'll never get to know God better.

Lucy is unable to move away from that first kiss – it may be exhilarating but there is no depth to it. It may feel wonderful but she is not getting to know Henry any better.

The writer to the Hebrews says this: 'So let us stop going over the basics of Christianity again and again. Let us go on instead and become mature in our understanding. Surely we don't need to start all over again with the importance of turning away from evil deeds and placing our faith in God. You don't need further instruction about baptisms, the laying on of hands, the resurrection of the dead, and eternal judgement. And so, God willing, we will move forward to further understanding.'

If you have lost your first exhilaration – don't panic. It's not the same as losing your first love.

We can't live in the past God wants us to grow up. He wants us to know him as more than a heavenly provider. My daughter is nine – to her I am just a heavenly provider of peanut butter sandwiches and milkshakes. By the time she's thirteen I will expect her to make her own food. I will still provide it but she will be involved. However, we'll also be able to have a much deeper relationship, discussing things she likes and dislikes. (Hopefully she will *want* to converse with me as a teenager – at least when her friends aren't around!)

But you see the point. Relationships move on. They grow and develop. They can't stay on day one. You make a new friend who seems perfect in every way, but if you go deeper that's when you find they're human.

So it is with God. Look at how the Old Testament characters prayed – they wrestled, argued, haggled, journeyed, ranted – much of my prayer life has only consisted of please, thank you and sorry. But no relationship survives well without more depth than that.

What do you think?

Questions:
1. Do you have a time alone with God in the morning or evening? Or do you have other ways of staying in touch with God?
2. If God is everywhere all the time - do we need to have a separate quiet time?
3. I often get into a position to pray, say my formal prayer, then stand up and continue chatting to God in a more informal, relaxed way. What do you think of this?
4. Why do we close our eyes when we pray? Do we need to close our eyes to hear from God? Perhaps we can connect with God by looking around at people, nature, the newspaper, or passing traffic?
5. Do you feel able to wrestle and argue with God?
6. Did the clip make you think about anything else?

Title: Contact – Restless Hearts

Theme: Our hunger for something more

Bible refs: Genesis 2; Matthew 7 v 7

Location of clip: 54 mins 21 secs to 56 mins 32 secs

Film Description:
Ellie is a scientist who has spent many long days trying to make contact with someone out there. She has done this ever since she was a young girl. Then one day it happens. Contact is made and suddenly there is a mad rush to find out who's on the other end of the line. There are many Christian characters in this movie and many good moments of conversation and debate about faith and science.

Clip Description:
The crowds have flocked to the listening station in the desert where contact with the aliens has been established. All kind of religious nuts, spiritual seekers, hungry hearts and weird control freaks are there, all wanting to get in on the action - all wanting a piece of this extra-terrestrial pie. Ellie drives through them, looking a little shocked and somewhat bewildered at the sight of this strange seething mass of hopeful humanity, from Elvis worshippers to UFO Abduction Insurance Companies.
As the TV announcer says: 'Many have come to protest, many to pray, but most have come to participate in what has become the best show in town.'

Thoughts:
Bono, lead singer of U2 once sang, 'I still haven't found what I'm looking for…' I love that song – but I used to feel guilty about liking it. Surely as a Christian I have found what I'm looking for, I should stop being restless now.

But how many of us are satisfied? And are we really supposed to be? Augustine said, 'Our hearts are restless till they find their rest in thee.' Even Jesus said, 'Keep knocking, keep searching, keep asking…' Nowadays I realise why I'm still restless, still searching, still hungry. I have an imperfect relationship with God. The more I have the more I want, the more I discover, the more I realise there is to discover. In a nutshell – more is less.

want what Adam and Eve had. They had an uncomplicated relationship with their creator. They weren't hampered by sin, guilt, peer pressure or doubts. Theirs was a triumphantly straightforward meeting of minds. That's what I long for. I was made for that kind of relationship with God; and even though I'm getting to know God, even though I have access to him through Jesus, it's not the same is it? It's like looking through that murky window. There are streaks and imperfections. I'm hearing God on a very bad line.

When I watch that clip from *Contact* I realise we're all hungry for that. We all go running after the next big thing. The next, hopefully-instant solution to the nagging problem of that ache inside. Whether it's aliens, superstars, heroes or villains – we all go chasing don't we? Even in the church. The different fads come and go, and we all jump on those passing bandwagons.

St Paul had to tell the Corinthians to stop turning him and Apollos into superstars.

Have you ever wondered why it's so easy to become addicted? It's not difficult is it? Just do something enough times and you'll be hooked. Shopping, coffee, smoking, junk food, pornography, chocolate. It's so easy to get stuck on something. I guess this is so because we're all designed to be addicted, aren't we? We're designed to not be able to make it through the day without our fix of God. But life is complicated and we get confused about what will satisfy that hunger. So we run after the next new thing, and fill that space with the latest candy.

The truth is much simpler. Two people in a garden, spending time with the guy who made them, inspires them, accepts them and understands them. Now that hits the spot.

One day, one day...

Questions:
1. I suppose most of us travel through different phases in our lives. Times of satisfaction, times of restlessness. How are you at the moment?
2. When you are restless - what do you do to satisfy this?
3. Do you think that God may be making you hungry for more?
4. In a world where we all have busy lives, what does it really mean to seek more of God?
5. Did the clip make you think about anything else?

Title: Independence Day – As Long As You're Happy…

Theme: Happiness, purpose and fulfilment

Bible refs: Matthew 5 vv 1-15

Location of clip: 1 hour 38 mins 40 secs to 1 hour 40 mins 25 secs

Film Description:
Gigantic spacecraft are on their way to earth and things don't look too dandy for the planet. Aliens have come to destroy the world. Los Angeles, Washington and New York are pretty much obliterated. America's in trouble and the whole of the planet is in great jeopardy. There's not much more to this one than that. The survivors desperately need some kind of counter-attack before it's all too late. One of them, ex-scientist David Levinson, gets to work on the problem.

Clip Description:
David is flat out on the floor, having fallen over from too much alcohol. The situation is too bad. He's given up all hope. How can they fight against such superior technology. There's just no way forward. His father comes to find him. He tries to encourage him.
'Don't give up,' he says, 'everyone loses faith at some point in their life…'
He confesses that he has lost faith, hasn't spoken to God since his wife died. But then he says, 'We have to remember what we still have.'
When David asks him what that is, his father flounders for a moment then replies, 'Well… you still have your health!'
And David laughs.

Thoughts:
'Just so long as you're happy and you've got your health, that's all that matters.'
We often hear that don't we. But how true is it? There are many healthy people out there who are desperately unhappy, and there are many unhealthy people who have a lot more peace than I have. Surely life isn't just about having your health and feeling good. If you're like me you need other things; purpose, fulfilment, job satisfaction, a sense of destiny, a sense that your life has greater meaning than just this moment, in this day, in this week.

Jesus outlined a different view on life when he delivered what we now know as *The Beatitudes*. He wasn't saying we have to deliberately be poor, persecuted, miserable and downtrodden, but he did bring a whole new perspective. In those days if you were rich and healthy you were

107

obviously favoured by God. (Sound familiar?)

But Jesus came along and said, 'Wait! Think again!'

It's not only the healthy and happy who are favoured – if you're poor, broken, sick and dying – God is still on your side. You can still know peace and fulfilment, happiness and hope.

That's why the disciples were so shocked when he said, 'It's very hard for a rich man to enter the kingdom of heaven!'

This would be like Jesus saying to us today, 'It's very difficult for a born again Christian to enter the kingdom of God.'

Like the disciples we would reply, 'Well who on earth can be saved then?' In their eyes to be rich was to be blessed. To have money was to have God on your side.

I have had the privilege of visiting slums in Cambodia and Kenya and I would say quite categorically - 'money doesn't buy you happiness'; in the same way that poverty doesn't indicate some kind of punishment.

In the clip David's father says: 'Everybody loses faith sometimes.' Well that's true. David's father is a Jew and the Jewish story is littered with men and women who lose faith, find it again, squander it, share it, bottle it up and spew it out again. Paul describes faith as perhaps one of the greatest commodities in life, alongside hope and love.

Perhaps these three are also important alongside health and happiness? What do you think?

Questions:

1. Tony Hancock once said that he didn't think it was possible to be happy in this life. What do you think? Do you know any continually happy people?
2. Jesus said, 'Where your treasure is - that's where your heart will be.' What matters to you most?
3. There are many more poor Christians in the world than rich ones. What do you think about that?
4. Have you experienced times of being poor, unhappy, lost or grieving - and yet found some kind of blessing in that?
5. Did the clip make you think about anything else?

Title: Bruce Almighty – You're Not Doing Your Job!

Theme: Being honest with God

Bible refs: Lamentations 3 vv 1-24

Location of clip: 20 mins and 5 secs to 22 mins and 32 secs

Film Description:
Bruce is on a bad day. He's been sacked from work, he was beaten up as he left the company car park and now his girlfriend Grace is giving him spiritual platitudes.

She is also trying to get him to pray about his problems, and to that end has got the children she teaches to make him some prayer beads. So Bruce decides to risk it and have a pray. However, beginning to communicate with God creates more trouble than he bargained for. Bruce discovers there's more to God than just a heavenly provider. God wants a proper relationship, with tough questions, hard dialogue and genuine responsibility.

Clip Description:
Bruce is driving in his car when he notices the prayer beads his girlfriend Grace gave to him. So he decides to pray. He takes them off his rear view mirror and starts to ask for a miracle to sort out all his problems. However, before he can finish he drives over a crater in the road and the prayer beads leap out of his hand. While he is fishing about for them under the seat he loses control of the car and drives into a lamppost. Bruce gets out of the car, takes one look at the damage and goes ballistic. He hurls the prayer beads into the river and shouts at the sky.

'Okay pal,' he says, 'the gloves are off... Smite me oh Mighty Smiter!'
Bruce is not happy and he's not going to pretend that everything's okay.

Thoughts:
Bruce does a dangerous thing – he tells God the truth. He lets out all the angry poison from inside and pours out his wrath on his maker. He's not going to pretend his life is okay. He hates what's happening, and as far as he's concerned it's God's fault. God is picking on him, God is making his life tough, and he could fix it all in five minutes if he wanted.

What Bruce doesn't realise is that this kind of thing is exactly what God wants. Real communication. Bruce has come out of hiding at last and is starting to tell God what's really going on, God can do nothing now but take him seriously. Before long Bruce finds himself in a warehouse talking to the big man himself. His life will never be the same again.

It's worth noting that when Bruce makes his first attempts at praying he does what most of us do. He sees God as a big Mr Fixit. He asks for a miracle so that he can just carry on with his life the way it was before everything fell apart. But God won't let him get away with that. He wants to be far more than just a magician. So, once Bruce starts praying honestly, he invites Bruce to come and see him.

It's a funny thing that, although we know God sees us as we really are, when we approach him we often put on a show. We're afraid to tell it like it is. We feel we must make vain attempts to be holy or spiritual in his presence. Even though he knows the muddled mess that we are. The Bible clearly demonstrates that we can come to God and let it all out. Jeremiah, not the greatest of party animals, let out all his frustration and bitterness when he wrote the third chapter of his diary, now known as Lamentations. He wasn't afraid to do that and once the poison was out he could see a little more clearly, he could honestly remind himself that in spite of appearances, God is good, and each day is a gift from him.

Questions:
1. Do you have many bad days like the one Bruce is having?
2. Do you feel able to talk to God about your anger?
3. How can we make church a place where we are more honest, not just coming out with the same glossy prayers and happy answers?
4. Have a look at some of the psalms and consider the way they 'tell it like it is'. Try psalm 31 vv 9-18, or psalms 35 and 38.
5. Did the clip make you think about anything else?

Title: Millions - Money Makes The World Go Around

Theme: Money

Bible refs: Matthew 6 vv 19-24

Location of clip: 14 mins 46 secs to 18 mins

Film Description:
Damian and his brother Anthony have recently lost their mum. They miss her terribly. The countdown is on to E day – the day when the pound will go and the Euro will come in as the common currency. Then one day, while Damian is sitting inside the cardboard den he built by the nearby railway line, a bag of money comes flying out of nowhere and lands in his playhouse.

Clip Description:
The boys take the money home and count it in Damian's bedroom. They discover they have a quarter of a million pounds. They bring their friends round one by one and show them a little of it, explaining that they have a few hundred pounds, and giving them a little to keep them quiet. But what will they do with the money now? Spend it, or give it to the poor?

Thoughts:
Damian wants to give the money to poor people, his brother has other ideas. Money is a powerful thing, and like anything powerful, it can be used for great good or great evil.

Jesus spent a lot of time talking about money, not because he wanted us all to be poor, but because it's so powerful that it takes a certain kind of wisdom to handle it. In an ideal world money would serve people, but often it's the other way round. Money becomes the dominant force, and many people spend their entire lives worrying about, earning and saving money. Jesus was unequivocal when he says, 'Where your money is – that's where your heart is.'

Money gives us away, it tells everyone what we love. It has a big mouth. For example, I spend money on books and music and films. And chocolate.

It's worth noting too that Jesus talks about worry straight after talking about money, making the connection between loving things, serving money and worrying about losing them.

The problem is – we all need it, and at different points in our lives we all want it a lot more of it. Whether it's to buy bigger things, or to do new things. And, if money is around to be used, then there's very little wrong with that. The problem with money is it's difficult to handle.

I remember being asked once, 'How much money would you give away if you won the lottery?'

To which I said, 'More money than if I actually really did win the lottery.'

We all dream of having *just enough* but once you have *just enough*, it's easy to worry about losing it, or maintaining it.

Jesus told a telling story about the man who we now know as 'the rich fool' – his crime was not being rich – it was hoarding his money. It seems the best antidote to a lot of money is generosity. What do you think?

Questions:

1. It's often been said that the church is always asking for money. Do you agree?
2. You may be struggling for money at the moment, is this something you can talk about with others?
3. What clues does your money give you about where your heart lies?
4. Do you think we view money too negatively?
5. Did the clip make you think about anything else?

Title: Blade Runner – Attack Ships On Fire Off The Shoulder Of Orion

Theme: The mystery and awesome nature of God and his creation

Bible refs: Job 38 & 39; Psalm 104; Revelation 12

Location of clip: 1 hr 41 mins 35 secs to 1 hr 43 mins 8 secs

Film Description:

We're in the future again – and this time it's all about artificial human beings – replicants or 'skin jobs'. Scientists have constructed these replicants, but now find them to be a threat to humankind. The order has gone out to hunt them down and destroy them - before they get us. Deckard is a Blade Runner – a future cop whose job it is to track down these replicants. Deckard stalks the streets of a bleak, rain lashed city, a grim vision of the future. Four replicants from outer space have hijacked a ship and returned to earth. Deckard must track them down and destroy them.

Clip Description:

'I've seen things you people wouldn't believe. Attack ships on fire off the shoulder of Orion. I watched c-beams glitter in the dark near the Tannhauser Gate. All those moments will be lost in time, like tears in rain. Time - to die.'

So says replicant Roy Batty (no relation to Norah as far as I'm aware) just before he bows his head and shuffles off this mortal coil. Deckard watches and wonders. Deckard has never seen these things. As he slips away Batty opens Deckard's eyes, and ours to a world of mythical size and wonder. The very language he uses and the style of his delivery makes it all seem dangerous and wonderful. There are things out there we just can't imagine. Batty gives us a brief glimpse of something bigger. Something 'other'.

Thoughts:

I love this little monologue – it's mythical – it gives you the sense that the world is much bigger than you ever imagined. What strange and awesome things are out there? Things our minds can't begin to grasp. It's said that there are places on this earth we never see. Ocean depths. Mountain tops. The inside of volcanoes. Places of fearful power and deadly creativity. There are creatures we can't imagine. Plant life we cannot touch.

We get a similar picture from the last four chapters of Job, or Psalm 104, or Revelation 12. You get a glimpse of a much bigger God, a massive world out there that's beyond comprehension. In Revelation 12 we see

God's perspective on Christmas. And instead of a little baby in a manger with shepherds and a few donkeys, there's a dragon, and a woman fleeing, there's danger and evil, vulnerability and a cosmic clash. Sometimes we need to remind ourselves that God is so much bigger than our ideas about him. Yes, he is the God who walks beside us, an arm around our shoulder, encouraging us, inspiring us, forgiving us, spurring us on. But he's also seen 'attack ships off the shoulder of Orion...' he's seen the universe. He's witnessed cosmic battles and universal upheaval; war in heaven and peace on earth.

When Job needs some perspective on life God points him to aspects of this world - but not the pretty flowers and gentle sunsets - he points him towards the awesome side of life. More or less saying - 'You are small Job, always remember this, there are things you will never fully grasp.'

In Genesis chapter 1 we see a God outside of time and space, calling planets and stars into being, decorating the chaotic void with life and colour.
In the very next chapter we see a God who walks on the earth, talks to people, shows them round. Makes them clothes when things have fallen apart. This is the mystery of our God. Big enough to squish stars in his fingers, small enough to sit beside us on a rock.

Mind-blowing, isn't it?

Questions:

1. Have you had any experiences that opened your eyes to the massive nature of God and his universe?
2. Have you read the last chapters of Job? They are strange and wonderful – what do you make of them?
3. How do you find having to live with the unknowable mysteries of God – the things beyond our understanding?
4. When he visited Athens Paul saw a statue dedicated to the unknown God and took the opportunity to introduce the locals to that God. People love mystery and myth – should we try and communicate more of this side of God's nature?
5. Did the clip make you think about anything else?

Title: Miracle On 34th Street – Signs And Wonders

Theme: God's desire to communicate with us

Bible refs: Hebrews 1 vv 1-3

Location of clip: 30 mins 54 secs to 33 mins 26 secs

Film Description:

Cynical mother Dorey Walker doesn't believe in Father Christmas. She is an executive at Macy's Department Store and it's her job to hire the actors playing Father Christmas in the different departments. Trouble ensues when she hires Kriss Kringle. The old man not only does a convincing job as the white bearded benefactor – he actually believes he really is the jolly man himself. He winds up in court – under threat of being locked away for being balmy! However a young lawyer defends him and producing a dollar bill reads the quote, 'In God We Trust.' This is a matter of faith – and he challenges the court on the whole question of belief. Meanwhile Dorey and her little daughter begin to believe in Father Christmas themselves.

Clip Description:

Kriss Kringle, a.k.a. Santa Claus, is doing his stuff in a big department store. Parents are bringing their children to him, to sit on his knee and tell him their Christmas lists. One mother brings her daughter to him, but when he starts to talk to her, the little girl's mother stops him and explains that she is deaf, and he need not try and communicate with her, she just wanted to see him.

Kriss looks carefully at her, thinks for a moment, then smiles. He begins to speak to her using sign language. She smiles and replies. They talk for a while and then end up signing *Jingle Bells* together. Kriss then glances across at another little girl, a rather serious child, who has been looking on longingly. Kriss winks at her and she quickly hides, realising that Santa Claus has spotted her.

Thoughts:

In amongst our many debates and much theological wrangling about God I wonder whether we forget one basic thing. God wants to communicate with us.

How can I say this when he's invisible and rather quiet at times? Suppose all those hunches, all those nudges and good ideas and moments of compassion and inspiration are coming from him?

Suppose his communication with us is like superfast broadband, the channels are always open and information is always flowing two ways. We

115

may give these things other names and descriptions, but it could be that God is a part of it all. Tom Shadyac, the director of Bruce Almighty once said that he thinks coincidence is God's way of remaining anonymous. I really like that.

Children often have an inbuilt sense of God and wonder and other worlds. Life can punch that out of us as we grow older. Jesus once pointed to a little child and said, 'Learn from them, become more like them, don't overlook their humility...'

In the church we can argue till the prodigals come home about the importance of various aspects of faith and theology – but we must never forget that behind everything - behind creation, the Bible, history and the present moment – is a God who made people so that he could be with them. Everything that happened in the Bible stemmed from the fact that God was always trying to get the attention of the wayward people he loved. When the folks in the Bible hit a crisis their response was to go back to the beginning, to revisit the creation story, to tell it again and remind themselves that at ground zero is a caring designer who communicates and is intensely interested in us.

Nowadays I have little time for formulas and instruction books that explain the latest theories about how to get God to do what we want him to do. It's so tempting to want to turn God into a vending machine, push the right buttons and he'll serve the right drinks. But let's stop that for a moment and try and see things from God's perspective...
I believe God often communicates with us through the ordinary things, through other people, through the practical workings of daily life, through nature and the city. We may look to God for specific guidance and answers to questions on our particular agenda, but he is always speaking to us about everything. About his nature and our nature, about the workings of normal life, and the struggles we face.

We often say that God is not Father Christmas, a benefactor with a big beard, but in the case of this scene I think we can safely say, he is just like Father Christmas, caring for this little girl and working hard to connect with her.

Questions:
1. Does God communicate with you in ways that others might find surprising?
2. Do you place less value on these forms of communication than the more conventional ones?
3. What kinds of things refresh your relationship with God?

4. Do you sometimes get cynical?
5. Did the clip make you think about anything else?

Title: Star Wars Episode 5: The Empire Strikes Back – First Impressions, Deceptive Can They Be

Theme: Learning from those older and wiser

Bible refs: Joshua 14 vv 6-14; Luke 2 vv 22-38

Location of clip: 52 mins 8 secs to 55 mins 19 secs

Film Description:
Episode 5 sees the evil Empire (surprise surprise) striking back. With the help of Darth Vader they attempt to wipe out the annoying rebels, a.k.a. Luke Skywalker and his sidekicks. The rebels are based on Hoth, and when the Imperial forces arrive to annihilate them, Han Solo and Princess Leia flee to Cloud City. Luke goes off on his own, looking for a little green, crinkled man called Yoda. Yoda is the Jedi's Jedi – the knight to top them all. Luke learns vital wisdom and he heads off to team up with the others to put a stop to Mr Vader and his naughty Empire.

Clip Description:
Luke waits in the swamp to meet up with Yoda. Yoda is right there with him, but he has no idea this is the great man. Yoda doesn't look like a top Jedi operative. He's small and green and talks funny does he. He's hardly a giant in his field. Yet this is the one who has trained Jedi warriors for 800 years. Appearances can be deceptive. Much more is there to tiny Yoda than meets the eye.

Thoughts:
Luke can't see past a little green man with big ears. He thinks he's hanging around with a muppet when in reality he's rubbing shoulders with a superhero. In this day and age of instant techno pop and torn designer jeans – the kids are kings. The young and the pretty are the new royalty. Everything panders to the naïve and inexperienced. They are the ones who matter. Yet history and the Bible teach us another lesson. The old and the grey have much to give us. They have lived and learnt. And we're deceived by their appearance. Life has left some of them looking a little ragged. They don't have green skin and ears like Spock – but they don't look like spiritual giants either. And many of them are. I remember someone telling me about their visit to meet Mother Theresa. They waited for a while in one of her hospitals and wondered where on earth this amazing woman was. Then they noticed a little cleaning lady, shuffling though the door. Except it wasn't just any cleaning lady - this was the woman who brought love to thousands and inspired millions.

It's easy to overlook people. We all do it. I heard recently that we make a judgement of someone within seven seconds of first meeting them.

Mary did it at the tomb. She looked at the grave-busting Son of Thunder and just saw a little insignificant gardener. Alan Titchmarsh instead of Jesus of Nazareth. She didn't recognise the man from God. Two guys walking to a place called Emmaus did the same thing. So did seven disciples in a boat.
The Bible is full of little wrinkled men and women who are dripping with wisdom and experience. Simeon and Anna, waiting patiently in the temple for a divine baby. Joshua and Caleb, men past their prime who invaded a land and gave birth to a nation. Abraham and Sarah, Elizabeth and Zechariah – way past their parenting days and yet suddenly producing offspring who would change the world.

But not all the old are wise. Many of the Kings featured in the book of… er… Kings went astray as they got older. Some of them began well – leading the nation along godly paths, but as their resistance dwindled and their eyes faded they took the wider roads, those that led to idol worship and compromise. Age and wisdom are not always good buddies. They say that youth is wasted on the young and age is a high price to pay for maturity. What do you think?

Questions:
1. Do you have older friends who have guided and encouraged you over the years?
2. We often hear of grandparents who prayed for years for member of their family – are you aware of older people praying faithfully in this way?
3. Have you ever looked to older friends for guidance and a listening ear?
4. Many churches have more older than younger people – why is that?
5. Did the clip make you think about anything else?

Title: Catch Me If You Can – Born To Run

Theme: Jacob the cheat

Bible refs: Genesis 27 vv 1-40

Location of clip: 17 mins 44 secs to 21 mins 47 secs

Film Description:
Frank W Abagnale was a conman. When his parents split up he ran away from home and little by little eased himself into a life of crime and deception. Brilliant and confidant he managed to pass himself off first as an airline pilot, then a doctor, and finally a lawyer. All without a single second of formal training. The story follows his life and the pursuit by the FBI agents who slowly closed in on him.

Clip Description:
It's Frank's first day as a student at a new school. He arrives nervous and tense and immediately feels out of place. When he enters his first classroom and is mocked by some of the students, he walks to the board, chalks his name up and announces loudly how it is pronounced. He then hurries the kids to their seats and begins to conduct their French lesson.

A week later his parents are called in when it finally comes to light that Frank is in trouble. Not because he has been skiving, but because he has been masquerading as a French teacher. He has already organised a parent/teacher consultation and was planning a trip to a French bread factory.
When his parents emerge from the headmaster's office his mother looks shaken, but his father glances at him and cracks a smile. He's a chip off the old block.

Thoughts:
Confidence will get you everywhere. If you stand tall and look as if you know where you're going you can pass through most doors marked 'private'. Frank certainly knew how to do that. And the Biblical Jacob was pretty good too.

Frank learnt his skills from his father, Jacob from his mother. It was Rebekah who set up the scam they played on his blind father, Isaac. When they dressed Jacob as Esau and tricked the older son out of the family blessing it was all her doing. Jacob was her boy, Esau was Isaac's lad. But it was Jacob alone who bartered a bowl of soup for his brother's birthright. Later, when it became clear that Esau hated his brother and intended to murder him, it was Rebekah who tricked Isaac into sending Jacob away. The mess of pottage was thickening all the time…

From then on, until the time when God gave him a limp, Jacob was always on the run. Just like Frank. He was ducking and diving, wheeling and dealing, sneaking his way in and out of trouble. And yet all the time God blessed him and looked after him. God had serious plans for Jacob. His name meant cheat – until the day of wrestling at the river Jabbok, when an angel ambushed him and his names was changed to Israel. One who wrestles with God.

Jacob went on to found a nation. Frank ended up working for the FBI. You never can tell the way things might work out.

Questions:
1. I once took cheat notes up my sleeve into a school exam, and on another occasion pretended I'd written a story penned by someone else. Do you think there's a conman inside many of us?
2. In spite of Jacob's cheating God was very much evident in his life. What do you think about this notion that God in his compassion can still work in us, in spite of our dodgy side?
3. When Jacob asked God to bless him, God gave him a limp – do you think God has ever blessed you with something that at first seemed negative?
4. Have you inherited any family traits?
5. Did the clip make you think about anything else?

Title: Matrix Revolutions – Stuck In The Middle

Theme: Caught between two worlds

Bible refs: Luke 9 v 28-36; John 11 vv 12-19; Philippians 2 vv 6-11

Location of clip: 7 mins 14 secs to 9 mins 53 secs

Film Description:
Part three of the Matrix Trilogy and there's one thing you can count on – it'll all be over in a couple of hours. People in black run a round a lot, on ceilings, pillars, cars and trains. There's an awful lot of shooting and astronomical phone bills. The Oracle has changed colour, Agent Smith's hiding inside some other guy and Neo's inside the Matrix even though he isn't *jacked in*. It's all one glamorous computerised circus. And it's loud enough to make your ears bleed. To be absolutely honest I have only a limited understanding of what it's all about or why it happens (a bit like life really) – but for the use of this clip you don't need to know. If you like sunglasses and bullets - enjoy.

Clip Description:
Neo wakes up and finds himself at Mobil Ave, a place neither inside or outside the Matrix. He is in a crossover place. A place where the two worlds meet. If you're going to take anything from one universe to the other than you have to do it through this place. He meets a family who explain this to him. Neo is astonished to discover that, although these people are just computer programmes they are acting out of love. Not only that, but they recognise that he is too.

Thoughts:
For thirty-three years Jesus inhabited a strange world like this one at Mobil Ave. He was very much human, very much of this earth. But he knew of another world. A place much larger, much freer than earth. He stood in the middle and brought the two together. It must have been a lonely place for him. He was seriously misunderstood. He just didn't fit in. He told stories people often derided or dismissed. He performed miracles as a sign, but people overlooked the signs and just put in a claim for a lot more of the miracles.

He had friends, but they often misunderstood him and in the end, rejected him. When he asked them on one occasion if they were going to leave him, along with the thousands of others who had turned away, they didn't say: 'No, of course not, we're your best mates.' They said, 'We can't think of anywhere else to go...' A kind of backhanded word of encouragement, I suppose.

On the mountain of transfiguration they got a glimpse of the real Jesus, this man caught between heaven and earth. On palm Sunday they saw it again. For a short time the people on earth recognised the man from heaven. Oddly enough the clearest glimpse they got lasted for six hours and it was the time he impersonated a criminal. On that occasion it was bloody and brutal and only two people spotted what he was up to - a Roman solider, hated by the Jews, and another criminal who was dying next to this man from another world.

He chose this mission because of love. Or perhaps he didn't choose – perhaps love has no choice. The God so desperate to nurture relationship with the world that he planned a covert invasion, disguised so well he looked just like you and me. And if that meant putting himself in a lonely place, straddling two worlds in order to bring peace, then he was prepared to do it.

Jesus's life was full of encounters like the one Neo has here. He met strangers all the time, and he always listened to them, respected them, and showed them love. He often engaged with women and children, unusual in his day. He even described children as great examples of what it meant to be God's people. As a bloke I'm not that inspired by the idea that I have to become childish to enter the kingdom, but maybe Jesus was speaking of their outspoken honesty, their thirst for knowledge, their uninhibited actions. Nothing seems dangerous to little children, they're not so bothered by peer pressure, life's an adventure and they often just say it like it is.

Do you ever feel caught in the middle yourself, out of place in this world? Jesus understands.

Questions:
1. Do you ever feel out of place, caught between two worlds?
2. Do you ever feel misunderstood by people close to you?
3. How do you treat strangers when you meet them?
4. Do you ever feel robbed of choice because of love? That you must do something because you care?
5. Did the clip make you think about anything else?

Title: Pretty Woman – No Easy Life

Theme: Life with God

Bible refs: Luke 14 vv 28-33

Location of clip: 1hr 49 mins 46 secs to 1hr 51 mins 41 secs

Film Description:
This is Cinderella by another name.

Edward is rich and ruthless. On a visit to Los Angeles he meets hooker Vivian and picks her up. However, Edward is lonely, and instead of the usual one night stand, he's looking for woman to spend a week with him. He needs a girl on his arm when he attends all those functions for the rich and famous. They haggle over the price and eventually strike a deal. Vivien spends a week living the high life. Edward discovers there's more to living than making money and dismantling other people's businesses.

Against all the odds they fall in love.

Clip Description:
This is the romantic climax of the movie. Just when Vivien thinks her dream lover has returned to reality and given up on her for good, a stretch limo rolls up outside her apartment and a handsome man in a grey suit steps out of the back seat. Richard has come back for her. He climbs the fire escape towards her window and she in turn leaps out and begins to climb down towards him. They meet halfway and, clenched in each other's arms, he says to her, 'So what happens when the knight rescues the princess?' And she says to him, 'She rescues him right back.'

Thoughts:
Richard turns up like a knight in a shining limo come to rescue Princess Vivian – and it all ends happily ever after. Or does it? Do we imagine for one minute that two people from different worlds can just kiss and make-up and ride off into the sunset.

These people come from entirely different solar systems. Richard's from the glamorous world of high finance, Vivian's from planet prostitute. Things may look rosy at this moment of much-kissing on the fire escape, but if Richard and Vivien are to have a real relationship there's an awful lot of hard work waiting for them round the corner. The kind of work that doesn't make exciting viewing… so, we won't bother with the sequel.

God turns up, not unlike Richard, or Prince Charming, or Shrek, and he climbs the fire escape and rescues us from that nasty tower and all those evil dragons. But if we think the relationship is going to be easy – we've got another think coming. We come from entirely different worlds. God and people have very different backgrounds. It's like trying to mix fire and ice. Somehow we have to work out how the two of us are going to live together. Perhaps that is why some people can't keep moving on with God, because the journey is not what they expected. Adjusting to life with God has many honeymoon moments, but there are also plenty of dark corners and unexpected turns in the road.

God is prepared for this, and it never surprises him.
Jesus advised his followers not to begin the journey until they had thought things through. 'No king goes to war,' he said, 'unless he is sure he can win.' This was a powerful picture for the people of his day, many of them wanted to go to war with Rome - an extremely difficult battle to win. 'Or,' he said, looking at Herod's attempts to win the people's favour by building them a huge Disneyland-style temple complex, 'no builder begins work unless he has worked out he has the resources for the job.'

Two very contemporary picture for the people of his day. He wanted them to think realistically about this *Pretty Woman* picture - God and people building a new life together.

Questions:
1. Have you been surprised by the nature of your journey with God?
2. What difficulties lie ahead in this parable of Richard and Vivien?
3. Are there parallels here with your relationship with God?
4. In an earthly relationship there are often recurring problems, do you find this in your relationship with God?
5. Did the clip make you think about anything else?

Title: Emma – 'Badly Done…'

Theme: Respect, criticism and encouragement

Bible refs: Philippians 2 vv 5-10

Location of clip: 1 hr 24 mins 53 secs to 1hr 29 mins 27 secs

Film Description:
Emma is a full-time matchmaker. She spends her days attempting to marry off her friends. However this often backfires on her. On route to mismatching many of her friends she discovers that she has fallen in love with Mr Knightley – her best friend. Oh dear. Can the great matchmaker make her own match?

Clip Description:
Emma and her friends are out on a picnic. A game is suggested. Each of them must say one very interesting thing, two mildly interesting things, or three very dull things. One of Emma's friends, Miss Bates, jokes that she will struggle to think of anything to offer, being of such humble mind.

Emma snaps back that Miss Bates's problem will be keeping the list of mundanities to just three things. There is an awkward silence as Miss Bates slowly realises the meaning of Emma's acidic comment.

Mr Knightley comes to Miss Bates's aid and rescues her from the embarrassment. Later, as they return home, Mr Knightley takes Emma to one side and chides her for picking on the lowly Miss Bates in front of everyone. Emma is clever and witty and privileged. Miss Bates is none of these things. 'Badly done, Emma,' says Knightley, 'badly done.'

And Emma turns away and hides her tears.

Thoughts:
Surely one of the greatest qualities we've lost in contemporary life is that of respect. It's a word we bandy around so much – as if saying it somehow confers it. But that's a lie. Respect is not a catch phrase. It's a state of mind. It goes along with humility, another quality you won't find much on our streets anymore.

In so much of life these days we're all talk, aren't we? Politicians, priests, believers and non-believers. We put slogans on police cars and adverts on buses. But at times the state of life declines, and communities splinter and fragment.

126

Respect is an unpopular idea. Humility is not applauded.

Except by God. He puts his hands together every time we look out for one another. Every time we listen to another and set them above ourselves the angels open another bottle of champagne. So much comedy and entertainment today is founded on pulling people down, and in some ways we deserve it, we have a celebrity culture where we love to watch unreal people being more and more destructive in front of a camera – a reality based on one-upmanship.

It's all a sham. Society cannot survive without respect and care for one another, corrupt regimes always collapse.

How do I measure up? Do I build others up, or tear them down?

It's worth noting that Jesus could humble himself because he was very sure of himself. Perhaps we find it difficult to humble ourselves now because so many of us have no idea who we are. We define our lives by comparing them with others. These verses from the letter to the Philippians are taken from a hymn (see Bible ref. above) and were included in the letter because in Philippi there were two classes of Christian - the haves and the have-nots. This song was a reminder to the rich Christians that Jesus made himself smaller, more humble, encouraging them to do the same.

We can be sharp-tongued and quick-witted, and I'm up there with the worst. But I know that on those few occasions when I lower myself and lift someone else up, somebody up there likes me. In the Message, Jesus is quoted as saying 'You care for others is the measure of your greatness.' What do you think?

Questions:
1. Sometimes it seems as if gossiping, backbiting and backstabbing are as prevalent in the church as they are outside of it. Do you think this statement is true?
2. We can't force others to be humble – we can only do that to ourselves. Frustrating, isn't it? What do you think?
3. Many of us complain about reality shows, yet we're still fascinated by them. I certainly am. What about you, do you get drawn in?
4. Who do you find it hard to respect?
5. Did the clip make you think about anything else?

Title: Grease – Don't Be A Fake

Theme: Being true to yourself, integrity and honesty

Bible refs: Psalm 139 vv 13-15

Location of clip: 22 mins 48 secs to 23 mins 24 secs

Film Description:
Danny and Sandy are in love. They meet during the summer vacation and have the holiday romance to end them all. When school starts up Sandy goes back to Australia and Danny goes back to being cool and hanging with his mates. However, they are both in for a shock. Plans change and Sandy ends up going to Rydel High, Danny's school. Before too long they will meet again, and then sparks will fly.

Clip Description:
Sandy joins a girl gang, the Pink Ladies, led by Betty Rizzo. When she talks about Danny Zucco, the love of her life, The Pink Ladies can't believe it. They know Danny – but he doesn't sound anything like the Prince Charming Sandy describes. So they take Sandy to meet Danny and she is in for a shock. At first Danny is overjoyed – he can't believe he is seeing his beloved Sandy again. Then he realises his friends are watching and suddenly he transforms into Mr Cool. He loses all sincerity and puts on a front. He's more concerned about what his mates will think than what Sandy feels. He bluffs his way along until Sandy accuses him of being a fake. She storms off with the other Pink Ladies, leaving Rizzo to stare long and hard at Danny. Rizzo knows what he's really like, she sees through his cover. Danny is a fake, he's trying to be cool, but underneath it – he's normal – and scared.

Thoughts:
Danny likes Sandy a lot. He doesn't really want to hurt her. But the peer pressure from his friends is too great. He wasn't emotionally prepared for this moment. Suddenly he's exposed, he runs for cover. He fakes being cool. It would cost him too much to be honest with Sandy in front of his friends.

Peer pressure dogs us all our life. As we grow up it turns into general conformity – but it's still peer pressure. We absorb the accepted forms of behaviour and forget who we really are. We learn how to cover up, which masks to put on to best suit each occasion. And some of those masks are Christian ones. We quickly learn how to behave in church – and we equate that behaviour with what is acceptable to God. Yet that's ridiculous. God sees us as we are – all the dark, restless, embarrassing thoughts, all the hours of heartbreak, every blundering moment.

He sees us when we're being honest and when we're faking it. And what's more he understands the pressures we are under. He knows why we fake it and he knows our weaknesses. Hebrews 4 verses 14-16 goes even further, it reminds us that that Jesus lived this life and experienced the pressures for himself. Psalm 139 describes us as complex people. This may explain why it's sometimes hard to understand ourselves or why we react in certain ways.

The truth about Jesus is that he is there in our moments of pretence, ready to help us discover reality and take a step towards genuine integrity. We don't have to be cool, competent or sorted out.
It's risky living, but in God we can find the grace to help us be ourselves.

Questions:
1. Vulnerability is not encouraged in our culture – how do we cope with this?
2. Often we need to be successful – in work and at church. What do you think of this?
3. Have you experienced moments when peer pressure has turned you into something of a fake?
4. Which kind of mask do you find yourself wearing most often?
5. Did the clip make you think about anything else?

Title: Jurassic Park 3 – God And Monsters

Theme: God is bigger than our ideas about him

Bible refs: Job 40 v 15 – 41 v 34

Location of clip: 21 mins 10 secs to 25 mins 16 secs

Film Description:
Dr Alan Grant agrees to return to Isla Sorna, the former breeding ground of all things prehistoric. He think he's just taking a wealthy adventurer and his wife on an aerial tour; what he doesn't know, is that they recently lost their son in a boating accident, and they've come to track him down. The usual carnival of raptors and T-Rex's come out to play, and our heroes spend the next 90 minutes screaming a lot and running from one bush to another.

Clip Description:
The group arrives on the island, only to be attacked by one of its green, scaly inhabitants. They try to take off but the plane crash-lands in a tree and before they can climb out, the monster is at them again, using the plane as its plaything, rolling it around with his foot. When the group tries and flees the monster chases them and they have to hide in the undergrowth. Just when they think they are safe a T-Rex raises its head nearby and they have to retrace their steps. Suddenly they find themselves caught between a rock and hard place – both of which have incisors the size of tombstones. Fortunately the monsters do battle with each other, rather than with the paltry humans that were originally on the menu.

Thoughts:
After Job and his friends have confused themselves and us with their many vain attempts to understand God a storm turns up. And along with the storm, the presence of God. Suddenly the earth trembles and all the discussion ceases, all their fancy ideas and clever theology crumbles in the presence of the one they're debating.

Malcolm Muggeridge once said, 'The Church is man's way of keeping God at bay.'
You could say that we see this principal at work here. There has been much discussion about Job and his pain, and his friends have presented many noble theories, but they have not made space for the one thing that can help them. God's presence with us through all of life.

They've been trying to explain things and demand answers from Job instead of looking for the one who can help them. Job and his mates are cornered by their own theology – they believe that if you are good you will be happy, healthy, prosperous and have a big family. Job has lost all these things yet he has not been bad. So the arguments and the explanations go on. They cannot make sense of it.

As the book draws to a close it's almost as if God cannot stay quiet any longer. He seems highly frustrated by all this impotent banter and so bursts on the scene with a whole host of special effects, including storms, hail, thunder and monsters.

'Okay! Okay!' he says. 'Enough already! Stop trying to second-guess me. I'm beyond your small thinking. Instead, here's an idea – open your eyes, look at the world. Move on from trying to box me – instead start to get to know me better.'
It seems to me that there is a big difference between getting to know God and trying to understand him. This ultimate creator, this being that is 'other' - different to anything our small minds may conceive.

God describes two great creatures in meticulous detail. Depending which version you read they're either the hippo and the crocodile, or Behemoth and Leviathan. Either way there's an awful lot of fine detail about them. God says take a good long look at what I've made. Some of it is not what you expect. Some of it is wild, dangerous, uncontrollable. Like me. Don't try and put me in a box, Job, I'll just chew my way out.

It is thought that Job may well be a play, and that it may well have been the first book of the Bible to be written down. If that is so it warms my heart. Job deals with the toughest question in life - why do bad things happen to us, do we cause them? Or is there a bigger more complex picture. And what is God like amidst the troubles. Jesus shook everyone up by rolling into town with his fistful of beatitudes, proclaiming, 'God is with the poor, the sick, the broken, the grieving, the lost.'

God is with us in our trouble, though we may fear we have been in some way cursed. In reality God never abandons us. Though life may be very hard indeed sometimes. Bono, the lead singer of U2 once said, 'God cares about the broken and the poor, and he is with us, when we are with them.'

In Ezekiel's book, in chapter 1, this reluctant prophet sees God and his vision is pretty strange, involving multiple-eyed winged creatures with more wheels than an articulated lorry. In chapter 4 God asks Ezekiel to deliberately defile himself by cooking over human faeces. Ezekiel protests, surely God doesn't want him, a priest, a holy man, to make himself deliberately sinful? But God's more concerned with communication than contamination.

In the next chapter God's at it again. 'Ezekiel – shave your head.'
In Leviticus 21 it's made clear that priests should never shave their heads – yet God says the opposite here. He's breaking his own rules. This time Ezekiel's got the point, he doesn't protest, he just gets out the Gillette.
A strange, otherworldly vision, a pile of human dung, and a spot of head shaving – let no one say you can out this God in a tidy, hermitically sealed compartment.

God is uncontainable. We may have our say about him, but God has the last word. Look at creation, open your eyes in the normality of life and we will see so many lessons, so many living sermons about God. So many messages from him coming at us on the airwaves of the ordinary, and yes – even through the hurricanes and the monsters.

Questions:
1. What do you think of when you consider the dinosaurs in the clip?
2. Have you taken time to learn something from God through animals, people or places?
3. What do you think about the notion of God having a wild side?
4. There are places on earth no one has ever seen. Yet they contain great beauty and intimacy. What does that say to you about God?
5. Did the clip make you think about anything else?

Title: Hotel Rwanda – Unspiritual Gifts

Theme: Gifts and talents

Bible refs: 1 Corinthians 12 vv 4-11; Matt 25 vv 14-30; Hebrews 11

Location of clip: 25 mins 40 secs to 28 mins 25 secs

Film Description:
This is the true story of Paul and Tatyana Rusesabagina. Paul was a hotel manager in Rwanda when the genocide began in 1994. The Hutu population rose up and began to slaughter the Tootsies. One million people died in 3 months – much of it encouraged via radio broadcasts. The radio presenters would announce where the Tootsi 'cockroaches' were gathered and instruct the Hutus to got out and 'cut down the tall trees'.

Almost against his better judgement Paul opened his hotel to local Tootsies as a safe house. He faced danger and death at every turn, but he took in more and more refugees until the place was full to bursting. Eventually he was able to transport them across the border to safety.

Clip Description:
Paul is a member of the Hutu tribe – but his family and friends are Tootsies. The soldiers have arrested them and are checking their ID cards to discover that most of them are Tootsi 'cockroaches'. The officer offers Paul his gun and tells him to shoot his own family. Paul says he can't use a gun. So the soldier demonstrates and hands it to him. Paul offers to pay money to free the hostages. The officer quotes a figure. The initial asking price is too high – Paul only has enough money to buy back his immediate family. Then he thinks again and offers to go the hotel to collect a lot more money to buy back everyone else. The officer considers this then agrees.

Thoughts:
After my wife, Lynn, and I watched this movie, Lynn said to me that she would never have thought to offer money to save lives in that situation. It just would not have crossed her mind. Paul Rusesabagina saved 1268 lives by bribing the Hutu soldiers.

As the movie progresses we discover that bribery is something Paul is well used to, he has a knack for it. When he first fell in love with his wife Tatyana she was working in a hospital, so he bribed a hospital official to move her to a different job nearer to him. Who would have thought that God would have used this unsavoury talent to save 1268 people's lives.

133

But he did.

I realise this is dodgy territory - as nobody wants to advocate bribery as a way of life. Yet there is no doubt that sometimes in life God uses the unexpected things we have to enable us to help others.
In Cambodia, during the terror of the Khmer Rouge era (1975-1978), a Christian school teacher stayed alive by posing as a fortune teller, an idea that popped into her head as she was praying for help when faced with death.

I used to think that God just wants to use the acceptable, 'Christian' bits of my life. Then I heard writer and speaker Adrian Plass say, 'Bring all the bits of your life to God and you may be surprised by what he does with them.'
Sometimes the notion presented is that God will clean up all the bad bits of our life and then use a happy, shiny version of ourselves to change the world. This is really not the case. Oscar Schindler, Bob Geldof and Mother Theresa were certainly not shiny, happy people and yet God made incredible use of them.

The heroes of our faith, as listed in the blog of Hebrews, post 11, were a bunch of dysfunctional misfits. We can take heart from God's call on their lives. Moses, the murderer, Abraham the liar and coward, Samson the spoilt brat, Jacob the wide-boy and wheeler-dealer.

In Matthew's blog, post 25, Jesus tells a story about 3 guys who are given gifts and then sent away to make the best use of them. It's a tale of innovation, competition and initiative.

So I wonder what 'gifts' we might have tucked away that we don't consider useful to God because they seem unspiritual. Paul only listed nine gifts in 1 Corinthians 12. But let's face it – we all possess a whole host of talents. Whether there are a first and second division of more and less spiritual gifts I don't know. But one thing's for sure, the world might be a different place if we brought those 'unspiritual' gifts to God for him to use.

Questions:
1. We often think that we need to be more spiritual to be better Christians. But perhaps we just need to bring all our gifts to God for his use. Have you ever done that?
2. Jesus told a parable about three men who were given gifts. Two of them used them well, the third buried his gifts. For this he was severely punished. Why do you think Jesus told this story?

3. We remember Joseph as a gifted dreamer – but he was equally gifted as an administrator – and it was ultimately this gift that saved Egypt and the surrounding countries from slow death by starvation. What gifts do you have? Think about this carefully, modesty often holds us back from identifying our strengths, but we all have them.
4. Take a moment to offer your gifts, talents and abilities to God, whether they feel spiritual or unspiritual.
5. Did the clip make you think about anything else?

Title: The Bourne Identity – Who Are You?

Theme: Identity

Bible refs: 2 Corinthians 5 vv 17-21; John 13 v 3; 1 Peter 2 v 9

Location of clip: 12 mins 58 secs mins to 17 mins 10 secs

Film Description:
Jason Bourne wakes up in a fishing boat with two bullets in his back and a number on a capsule buried in his leg. He has no idea who he is or where he's come from. He sets off to find himself (literally) and discovers that he must find out his true identity if he is to survive. Unknown killers are on his trail; and things are looking very bad.

Clip Description:
Jason enters a Swiss bank in search of the safety deposit bearing the number he found in his leg. When he finds this and opens it he discovers that he has an awful lot of money, some guns and ammo and a dozen different identities. He is any number of people and has several different nationalities. He has narrowed the field but still has no real idea of who he is or where he's come from.

Thoughts:
When Jesus knelt in the dust to clean the muck and the grime from the disciples' feet he knew who he was. He was secure in his identity and his place in the world. The knowledge freed him up, he didn't need anyone else to tell him he was the king of the world.

The Bible describes us in terms that seem almost laughable. Apparently I have royal blood, I'm holy, and I'm pure and faultless. Try telling my wife that! We live with two realities, don't we? Our place in the universe and our place in God's kingdom. I don't understand this, and I do think there is a danger of using it for spiritual escapism. This life is tough so let's just imagine ourselves somewhere else nice and holy. But it doesn't mean that. Let's face it, I'm sat here in Devon in my pyjamas, surrounded by chaos and boxes, not seated in some other realm somewhere.

It was Moses who first coined the phrase about being different. He recorded this message to the people from God in his Exodus blog, post 19:
'Now if you will obey me and keep my covenant, you will be my own special treasure from among all the nations of the earth; for all the earth belongs to me. And you will be to me a kingdom of priests, my holy nation.'

Peter, Jesus's best mate, then remixed it and wrote it for the rest of us. 'And now God is building you, as living stones, into his spiritual temple. What's more, you are God's holy priests, who offer the spiritual sacrifices that please him because of Jesus Christ.'

This is very much about being God's reps on earth now. The temple was thought of as God's home on earth. Well, says Pete, people are now God's home on earth. People viewed by God as precious, holy, different, unique.

The Bible does not take the line that the spiritual and physical should be separated out, far from it, it claims that the two are deliberately and inextricably linked. Instead it suggests that our place in God's sight can help us find our place in our own eyes.

Jesus always held lightly to the praise others gave him, no doubt he appreciated affirmation and was hurt by accusation, but ultimately he was clear about the person God had made him. He came from his father and was headed back there, and along with that, he was king of the universe. This liberated him from two things. One - the constant need for others to affirm him, and two - the search to find himself. In John 13 we are told that Jesus knew he had come from God, was going back there, and had complete authority on this earth. He probably discovered a lot about this three years earlier when he had his desert experience, and we often find out a lot about ourselves in the dark, dry places.

Did this knowledge of who he really was make him seek a life of privilege? Not at all. It enabled him to bend down beside cruddy, smelly feet and carefully wash them clean. A job usually done by unclean gentile slaves. The lowest of the low.

Knowing who he was turned Jesus into a servant. And this incident was not long after he had ridden into Jerusalem on a donkey while crowds had hailed him king. If that was me in front of those cheering crowds it would have gone to my head. But not Jesus, he probably enjoyed the Palm Sunday moment, but he didn't base his identity on the cries of a crowd. Jesus was not fooled by the X Factor moment.

Questions:
1. What defines you? Where do you get your identity?
2. Do you get glimpses, as Jesus did, that you have come from God and are going back to him? Are there others who have helped you see this reality?
3. Have you ever been lifted by the applause of others, and then struggled because of it later on?
4. Have you ever lost your sense of identity – perhaps through moving house, changing jobs, becoming a parent, retiring, getting married

or divorced or widowed?

5.　Did the clip make you think about anything else?

Title: Bridget Jones's Diary – Flailing In The Dark

Theme: Reality and weakness

Bible refs: 2 Corinthians 12 vv 7-10; 1 Timothy 1 vv 15&16

Location of clip: 1hr 6 mins 40 secs to 1hr 8 mins 30 secs

Warning: This clip contains one barely distinguishable swearword

Film Description:
Bridget Jones is 31, single and lonely. She keeps a diary and monitors her cigarettes, calories and conquests. She resolves to improve her life – but it all goes badly wrong when she falls for her boss, Daniel Cleaver. Cleaver is a womaniser and a general wide-boy and before long it becomes clear that he's playing fast and loose with Bridget's heart. In the meantime Bridget is nurturing a growing disgust for family friend Mark Darcy, whom she greatly distrusts. What she doesn't realise is that Darcy is actually a nice guy – and one who is slowly falling in love with her.

Clip Description:
It's crunch time – Darcy and Cleaver are fisting it out on the pavement. They hate each other and both want Bridget for themselves. They fight like big girls, with much leg flailing and hair pulling. They are not battling like Brad Pitt or Tom Cruise. These are men who are not well-versed in the art of street fighting. There is a great moment when the fight invades a nearby restaurant and they stop throwing punches in order to sing Happy Birthday. Only in England.

Thoughts:
Life is rarely like the movies really. If you're depressed on screen then Simon and Garfunkel, or Coldplay will be playing softly and perfectly in sync in the background. If you're happy you'll be able to run up to total strangers and kiss them. If you're leg hurts you'll be able to accurately diagnose that it's broken. At night when you put the light out the dark always has a nice blue tint to it. When you fight someone you'll be able to deliver jackhammer punches that will always find their mark and never break your hand.

Except in this movie.
Mark Darcy and Daniel Cleaver attempt to fight like men and end up flailing about desperately trying to do each other damage.
So much of my Christian life feels like this – flailing about in the dark, trying to swing punches and triumph over disaster – and much of the time I

look completely ridiculous. I try and pretend I'm together, I'm cool and I have a confident 'Christian' life. But the opposite is true. I could well put my hand up with Paul and proclaim, 'Look at me – I'm the biggest sinner around.'

Thank goodness that God uses us in our mess and weakness – because I have that stuff in spades. How about you?

Questions:
1. Ever feel like you make a mess of your 'Christian' life? Do you think of part of your life as 'Christian'?
2. There is much talk about triumphant Christian living. I know of no one who lives this kind of life. In fact I believe it's an unreal, idealised view of life. What do you think?
3. After seven chapters of encouraging the Romans to live well, Paul confessed he was a big sinner. His response was then to say, 'Thanks be to God, because Jesus helps me.' How does he help you with your failure and brokenness?
4. Can we be more honest about our muddled lives? Is it possible, or does it leave us too vulnerable, too exposed?
5. Did the clip make you think about anything else?

Title: Touching The Void – If You're Going To Die, Die Climbing

Theme: Keep moving on with God

Bible refs: Joshua 14 vv 6-15

Location of clip: 18 secs to 3 mins 3 secs

Film Description:
This is the true and remarkable story of Joe Simpson's journey back down Siula Grande peak, with a badly broken leg and a shattered ankle. He and fellow climber Simon Yates had reached the summit, in the Peruvian Andes, and were on their way back down when Joe slipped, smashed his leg and fell down a crevasse. Simon, thinking his friend was dead, cut the rope and ventured back to base camp, alive but devastated. Joe meanwhile, endured the pain and began the long slow crawl back down the mountain.

Clip Description:
This is the opening credit sequence – the introduction by Joe and Simon to their catastrophic climb. Joe talks about their passion for climbing, they were reckless, daring, anarchic. Climbing was fun to them, the mountains a challenge that they faced with energy and wit. They weren't going to be cowed by the size of the climb. The enormous challenge of it was just what appealed to them.

Joe has slipped off the mountain and fallen into the crevasse. He is alone now, Simon cannot find him and believes there is no way he could have survived. Joe lowers himself onto what he thinks is the floor of the crevasse. He soon discovers it is only a wafer-thin shelf, and that too much weight and too much movement will smash the icy floor and spell death for him. Inch by agonising inch he crawls across, and slowly, very slowly he climbs up the opposite wall and eases his way out of the crevasse through a tiny hole. Every step puts pressure on his broken leg, but he can't think about that, he can only concentrate on climbing.

Thoughts:
Life throws us any number of mountains to climb. Some we can choose to go round, some we avoid for a while, some we just have to don the gear and start going up. In her song *I Hope You Dance*, Leanne Womack offers us the line ' I hope you never fear those mountains in the distance, never settle for the path of least resistance.' That's something Caleb, in the book of Joshua, would certainly concur with. 'Give me that hill country,' he says. I want a challenge.'

141

Caleb is extraordinary in his courage, daring and good humour. After years of desert living, after months of battling, after the disappointment of not getting in to the promised land the first time, he still wants more. He still wants that challenge that was once promised to him. Let me at them hills – I'll take the tough country all right!

This is not *Last of the Summer Wine* territory. Caleb won't be happy seeing out his days wandering around reminiscing. He wants to forge onward. Keep climbing. Battle the giants.
If only I was like that. I'll avoid the problems if I can. If it's a toss-up between a molehill and a mountain – I'll take the molehill anytime thanks.

In his book, *Risky Living*, Jamie Buckingham wrote this – If a man is going to die, let him die climbing. Well, we all of us will die, and we all of us face mountains. Maybe somehow we can pluck up a little more courage and pick up that pickaxe. Maybe right now, we have little choice anyway. The reality is that for most of us mountains aren't an optional extra, they're part of the journey. They just lie there on route, waiting for us. So what helps us? What helps you climb the mountains?

My problem is I'm like the guy who came to Jesus and said 'I believe, help me with my unbelief...'
I know the theology and the theories, and I have some courage – it's just that I need a lot more. Because I also have a huge stack of fears.

What do you think?

Questions:
1. What sort of things encourage you to keep going?
2. Do you know older Christians who are still growing in their faith?
3. Does church keep you growing – does it push you forward with God?
4. The fear of persecution has been a big shadow in my life for a long time – the book of Revelation is no bundle of laughs for me. Are you able to talk to others about some of your fears? Can you pray about your fears with others?
5. Did the clip make you think about anything else?

Title: Toy Story – The Secret Life Of Christians

Theme: Witnessing and the Christian life

Bible refs: Luke 24 vv 44-49; 2 Corinthians 4 v 7

Location of clip: Start of film to 7 mins 43 secs

Film Description:
Andy is a boy of many toys. He loves them all and plays with them regularly. What he does not realise is that when he is out of the room they come to life and have a secret existence all of their own. They walk, talk, laugh, argue, fight and play, all under their own steam. Andy's favourite toy is Woody, a cowboy who also happens to be in charge of all the other toys when he's not around. But when Andy gets a new Buzz Lightyear for his birthday, Woody's place as top toy comes under serious threat. Buzz is far more sophisticated and can do many more things than Woody. All is not well in the playroom.

Clip Description:
This is the opening sequence. Andy plays with his toys – Mr Potato Head and Woody have a gunfight. When his mum calls him Andy runs off and leaves the toys. When all is quiet in the playroom Woody opens one eye, then the other, then stands and gives the all clear. Toys wake up all over the playroom and suddenly we see them in their true light. These toys have a life of their own. Andy convenes a meeting to discuss the fact that they will soon be moving house. Also on the agenda is Andy's birthday party, happening later that day. The toys panic about this, they are always worried that new toys will replace them in Andy's life. This is the secret life of toys, the life we humans never get to see.

Thoughts:
I often feel as if I live two lives. When I'm out and about in the world I operate one way, when I'm in a Christian gathering I operate in another. I know it shouldn't be like this – but I can't help it. In a Christian setting I discuss things and experience things I don't when I'm outside. I hear talks and sing songs that probably would not make a lot of sense to many people in the wider world. And I wonder how they would view me in my Christian guise. I have a whole other life going on which the world is unaware of.

It's like the Toys – as far as the Children are concerned they operate in a rigid, wooden, lifeless fashion. They do and say a few limited things but that's about it. The children have no idea that when they're alone, the toys talk and act, sing and dance, laugh and joke and have crazy adventures. Not unlike us Christians. We have a whole other world going on and it's so difficult to explain this to other people. They see one side of us as Christians, wooden, stilted, limited. It's portrayed on TV and in newspapers, and it's unreal to them. I noticed the comedy series Rev is back on TV - I like that because it portrays a Christian couple in a much more real, earthy way.

How can we help those outside see the reality of our lives as Christians? Do we want to?
The toys are quite happy to hide away and keep their other life secret. We have a problem with that. We've been commanded to expose people to the other side of life. Before Jesus came the Jews often kept their faith to themselves, an exclusive religion. But Jesus told us to turn it inside out. Don't be exclusive, be inclusive.

So what helps? What doesn't help?

Questions:
1. I think that some of the songs and language we use in church do not help us connect with those outside. What do you think?
2. How do you feel when you bring strangers into your church or Christian meeting?
3. Which bits of your faith would you most like to expose to those people you know who are on the outside looking in?
4. Which bits would you definitely not like them to see?
5. Did the clip make you think about anything else?

Made in the USA
Charleston, SC
16 April 2013